Beyond Redistribution

Beyond Redistribution

White Supremacy and Racial Justice

Kevin M. Graham

LEXINGTON BOOKS
A division of
ROWMAN & LITTLEFIELD PUBLISHERS, INC.
Lanham • Boulder • New York • Toronto • Plymouth, UK

Published by Lexington Books
A division of Rowman & Littlefield Publishers, Inc.
A wholly owned subsidiary of The Rowman & Littlefield Publishing Group, Inc.
4501 Forbes Boulevard, Suite 200, Lanham, Maryland 20706
http://www.lexingtonbooks.com

Estover Road, Plymouth PL6 7PY, United Kingdom

British Library Cataloguing in Publication Information Available

Library of Congress Cataloging-in-Publication Data
Graham, Kevin M., 1968–
  Beyond redistribution : white supremacy and racial justice / Kevin M. Graham.
    p. cm.
  Includes bibliographical references and index.
  ISBN 978-0-7391-3096-4 (cloth : alk. paper) — ISBN 978-0-7391-3098-8 (electronic)
  1. Racism. 2. Whites—Race identity. 3. White supremacy movements. 4. Distributive
justice. I. Title.
  HT1521.G675 2010
  305.8—dc22   2009042674

The paper used in this publication meets the minimum requirements of American
National Standard for Information Sciences—Permanence of Paper for Printed Library
Materials, ANSI/NISO Z39.48-1992.

Printed in the United States of America

To the leaders of Omaha Together One Community,
without whose research, discussion,
agitation, organization, and action
this book would never have been written.

Table of Contents

Acknowledgments

Much of the research for this book was carried out with the support of a Summer Faculty Research Grant from the Creighton University Graduate School, for which support I am very grateful. The Graduate School also provided crucial support and encouragement for the completion of this project by allowing me to participate in a Seminar for Mid-Career Scholars led by Bridget Keegan. Special thanks go to the staff of the Historical Society of Douglas County (HSDC) Library and Archives Center for their help in utilizing the archives of the *Omaha World-Herald*, which they administer. Documentation of many historical aspects of race relations in Omaha would have been impossible without the hard work that the paid and volunteer staff of the HSDC have put into creating and maintaining the vertical file of *Omaha World-Herald* clippings.

Earlier versions of several chapters of the book were published in a variety of places. An earlier version of chapter three was published in *Social Theory & Practice* 26, no. 2 (2000); an earlier version of part of chapter four was published in the *Journal of Value Inquiry* 36, no. 1 (2002); an earlier, significantly different version of chapter five was published in *Public Affairs Quarterly* 15, no. 3 (July 2001); and an earlier version of chapter six was published in *Social Philosophy Today, Volume 16: Race, Social Identity, and Human Dignity*, ed. Cheryl Hughes (Charlottesville, Va.: Philosophy Documentation Center, 2002). These chapters are reprinted by kind permission.

The book has benefited immensely from the comments and criticisms voiced by audiences at a variety of conferences, including the annual International Social Philosophy Conferences sponsored by the North American Society for Social Philosophy and the annual Central and Eastern Division Meetings of the American Philosophical Association. My presentations to these conferences would not have been possible without the generous support of numerous Faculty Development Travel Grants from the Creighton College of Arts & Sciences.

Various chapters of the book have benefited from the comments and criticisms of colleagues around the US and Canada, including Marilyn Friedman, Alistair Macleod, Charles W. Mills, John Rowan, and Lisa Schwartzman. I owe special thanks to colleagues who commented on my presentations of early versions of various chapters of the book to annual meetings of the Canadian Philosophical Association, the Central Division of the American Philosophical Association, and the Eastern Division of the American Philosophical Association, including Joel Anderson, Howard McGary, Margaret Moore, and Tim Sommers. Howard McGary, in particular, helped me to see the issues that I address in chapter four in an entirely new light.

My philosophical colleagues at Creighton University have served as an exemplary community in which to think philosophically about the practical and theoretical issues of racial politics addressed in this book. I would like to thank personally J. J. Abrams, Angela Batson, Jack Carlson, Elizabeth Cooke, Randy Feezell, Patricia Fleming, Fr. Tom Krettek, S.J., John O'Callaghan, William Stephens, and Richard White for their comments, criticism, advice, and support. Special thanks go to Patrick Murray, Deirdre Routt, and Jeanne Schuler, all of whom read and offered comments and criticism about every chapter of this book, often more than once. I cannot imagine having written this book without the support of any of the three of them.

Introduction

I began to recognize white supremacy while sitting in a pew of St. Paul African Methodist Episcopal (AME) Church in Cedarville, Ohio. I was a child of grade school age attending a community Lenten worship service sponsored by the town's ecumenical ministerial association. My father was serving as pastor of the United Presbyterian Church in Cedarville, and he took his commitments to the ministerial association pretty seriously. So, every Wednesday in Lent each year, our family attended the weekly community worship service that was hosted in rotation by the town's congregations of the African Methodist Episcopal Church, the Church of God, the Nazarene Church, the United Methodist Church, and the United Presbyterian Church. We were joined each week by a number of other families from various congregations who attended virtually every week of every Lenten season and by some members of the host congregation who would attend only the service hosted by their home church each year.

The only break in this regular pattern of attendance at the community Lenten services came when the weekly service was hosted by St. Paul AME Church, the only predominately African-American congregation in our predominately white town. Every year, when my family attended the community Lenten service at St. Paul AME Church, we were the only white family present. Not one white member or pastor of the other five predominately white congregations represented in the town's ministerial association ever attended a community Lenten service hosted by St. Paul AME Church in all the years I lived in Cedarville. The only others present were members of the host congregation, who were African-American.

The makeup of the congregation was not the only thing that struck me about the services hosted by St. Paul AME Church. The style of worship in general, and the music in particular, were quite different from the worship and the music employed by all of the five predominately white Protestant churches where we worshipped during Lent, although those five churches ran the gamut from mainline Protestant to charismatic Pentecostal in their theology and their liturgy. The church building also appeared run down and in need of repair, from the peeling white paint on the outside of the building to the worn, wooden floorboards inside. Yet the most vivid impression that I recall from my worship experiences at St. Paul AME Church can be summed up in the question, "Where are all the other white people?"

My adult efforts to analyze white supremacy from a philosophical perspective are, in some sense, an attempt to digest my lifelong experience with white supremacy in the United States, which began in a pew of St. Paul AME Church. Some aspects of white supremacy that were visible from my pew in the church, such as the peeling paint and the worn floorboards of the church building, were direct results of the unjust distribution of income and wealth along lines of race in the US. As I discovered during my doctoral studies in philosophy, political philosophers have devoted much time and effort in recent decades to developing theories of distributive justice that can adequately address these effects of white supremacy.

The more I studied the leading philosophical theories of distributive justice, such as that developed by the late John Rawls in *A Theory of Justice*, the more I wondered about their capacity to address other aspects of white supremacy that are not directly related to distributive injustice. Why didn't other white Christians in Cedarville attend the community Lenten services at St. Paul AME Church? Was there something fearful or loathsome about a space that is socially marked as black rather than white that kept the other whites away? Was the style of worship and music employed by the African Methodist Episcopal Church culturally marked as base or inferior by virtue of its association with African-Americans? Were the bounds of white Christian ecumenism stretched to breaking when an invitation to common worship came from a fellow Protestant congregation whose members happened to be African-American? Whatever the answers to these questions might have been, it was clear that among Protestant Christians in Cedarville, Ohio, there might be neither Jew nor Greek and neither slave nor free, but there certainly were black and white, and there was no question who was viewed as inferior and who as superior.

This book is an attempt to understand the aspects of white supremacy that are not obviously consequences of the relative affluence of whites and the relative poverty of non-whites. Can such aspects of white supremacy be explained completely by distributive theories of justice, or not? I argue that they cannot, but it will take me six chapters to establish this conclusion.

Some social and political philosophers approach race-related injustice from an ethical perspective and focus on racism as a moral vice. Others approach it from a social perspective and focus on racial oppression as an unjust political system. In chapter one, I argue that the concept of racism, on which the ethical perspective focuses, can explain only part of the full range of forms of race-related injustice. I maintain that the full-range of race-related injustice is better accounted for from the social perspective, analyzing racial injustice in terms of Charles Mills' concept of white supremacy.

A word of clarification about the term "white supremacy" is necessary here. By "white supremacy," I do not intend to refer exclusively or primarily to political movements such as the Ku Klux Klan or the Aryan Nation that expressly advocate for the privileging of whites over non-whites. Such political movements are now largely marginalized and unlikely to capture broad political support. I use the term "white supremacy" much more broadly to the institutions and practices that privilege whites over non-whites in the US and around the world. White supremacy in this broad sense need not be advocated or justified by white supremacist politics in the narrow sense in order to have the effect of privileging whites over non-whites. The concept of white supremacy is intended to direct our attention away from individual people's beliefs and attitudes, on the one hand, and toward social patterns of privilege and disadvantage, on the other.

The utility of the concept of white supremacy can be illustrated by examining the phenomenon of police violence against African-American men in the United States. I examine this national phenomenon in microcosm in chapter two by examining two recent cases where police officers killed African-American men in Omaha, Nebraska, the city where I now live. The traditional catalog of civil rights and liberties developed by liberal political philosophers over the past four centuries can account well for some of the forms of injustice involved in the killings, such as the police officers' violations of the victims' rights to life, liberty, security of the person, and equality before the law. What the traditional liberal account misses, however, is that the causes of these injustices do not lie at the ethical level of racist attitudes or beliefs of individual white police officers or public officials about nonwhite citizens, but at the social level of power relationships between whites and nonwhites. The concept of white supremacy can help us understand how the killings examined are part of a systematic pattern of unjust power relations rather than isolated, anomalous departures from the just functioning of a liberal democratic local government.

Contemporary liberal political philosophers, among others, have developed theories of social justice that aim to reveal systematic patterns of social injustice. The leading contemporary liberal approach to systematic injustice, whose preeminent advocate was the late John Rawls, maintains that systematic injustice can be analyzed in terms of unfair distributions of social resources. Communitarian and feminist critics of Rawls have charged that his distributive theory of justice is based on an inadequate conception of human persons as abstract individuals. I argue in chapter three that Rawls was right to respond that his critics misinterpreted his position. Rawls is, nevertheless, committed to a form of abstract individualism about human persons, although not in the way that many of his critics contend. Rawls's commitment to abstract individualism is not expressed by his abstract depiction of the parties to the original position in which principles of justice are chosen, but by his conception of social resources as objects that individuals can possess, use, exercise, or enjoy on their own. The commitment to abstract individualism prevents Rawls from giving a full account of certain forms of injustice suffered by members of minority cultures and members of subordinate races.

Moving beyond the work of Rawls in particular to examine contemporary liberal political philosophy in general, I follow Will Kymlicka in chapter four by arguing that liberalism in all its forms is fundamentally committed to making the achievement of autonomy available to individuals as a matter of social justice. Many contemporary liberal political philosophers, like Rawls and Kymlicka, have diverged from earlier versions of liberalism by interpreting the commitment to autonomy as a commitment to distribute fairly to all individuals the social resources required for the exercise of autonomy. Different varieties of contemporary liberalism are then distinguished from one another by how they define "autonomy," "individual," "social resources," and "fair distribution." Despite these differences, however, the fundamental commitment to a distributive account of the means to autonomy prevents contemporary liberal political philosophers who make this commitment from addressing some of the root causes of white supremacy, such as white supremacist controlling images of nonwhite persons. I argue that if liberals are to address the root causes of white supremacy using a theory whose central value is autonomy, then they will need to leave their commitment to a purely distributive conception of social justice behind.

A controlling image is defined by social theorist Patricia Hill Collins as being similar to a stereotype insofar as it offers a limiting, distorting, derogatory depiction of members of a subordinate racial group. But unlike stereotypes, controlling images are connected to rewards and punishments that are meted out to those members of the subordinate racial group who fill or fail to fill the role prescribed by the image. I argue in chapter five that white supremacist hate speech can express and entrench controlling images of nonwhites, and thus white supremacy, in a variety of ways. In this way, white supremacist hate speech causes serious harms to nonwhite persons, harms that liberals should take pains to redress or prevent. The state is therefore obligated to seek to eliminate racist hate speech through education and through the regulation of speech. I argue, however, that liberal political philosophers who operate within the distributive paradigm cannot endorse such a state obligation.

A reader might respond to my critiques of contemporary liberal approaches to addressing white supremacy by asking what alternative approach I have to offer. I sketch such an alternative approach in chapter six, which deals with white supremacy in US public education in the local context of Omaha public schools. The Omaha Public School board proposed to end desegregation busing in 1999 and to raise $240 million in tax dollars mainly to repair and replace aging school buildings in predominately African-American and Latino neighborhoods. The 1999 proposal marked a shift from an approach to ending white supremacy in public education through desegregation to an approach that aimed to do so through fair distribution of educational resources. I argue that the effort to end white supremacy in public education in Omaha by fairly distributing educational resources is incomplete because it fails to address the historic legacy of white betrayals of nonwhites and nonwhite distrust of whites in Omaha. I conclude that the pursuit of distributive justice must therefore be supplemented by efforts to create equal participation in deliberative democracy if educational justice is to be achieved.

I have written this book because I believe that the forms of social injustice related to white supremacy are not understood well by many social and political philosophers. I hope that the book will contribute to a better understanding of what white supremacy involves and what must be done to bring white supremacy to an end in the United States. Understanding white supremacy is a necessary step toward eliminating white supremacy from American society. It is not, however, by any means sufficient for the elimination of white supremacy. Even if white supremacy were completely understood, much difficult political work would remain to be done in order to eliminate it. The political work that would be required includes, but is not limited to, building personal relationships across lines of racial difference, organizing cross-racial coalitions to work towards realizing a common vision of racial justice, and acting collectively on the basis of such a vision. This book is dedicated to the men and women who devote themselves to doing this work, and particularly to my fellow leaders in Omaha Together One Community, from whom I have learned so much.

Chapter One
Racism or White Supremacy?
Understanding Race-Related Injustice

Whites and nonwhites are obviously situated quite differently in the United States today. For example, over 30% of African-Americans (as compared with less than 10% of white Americans) lived in poverty with respect to income in 1999, while 54% of African-Americans (as compared with 25% of white Americans) lived in poverty with respect to assets at the same time.[1] White American men are six times more likely to be sent to prison than to attend college or university in a given year, but African-American men are one hundred times more likely to suffer the same fate.[2] African-Americans' life expectancy is 6.6 years less than that of white Americans, and the rate of infant mortality among African-Americans is more than double the rate for white Americans.[3]

Not every difference between the social and economic standing of whites and nonwhites is the result of injustice, of course. Nevertheless, differences like those mentioned above are prima facie unjust, since no one deserves to be poorer, to have a higher risk of incarceration, or to be at greater risk of premature death simply because one is nonwhite rather than white. In the absence of good evidence to the contrary, then, it would appear that race-related differences like those mentioned above are due, at least in part, to race-related injustice. Different theories of racial justice will, of course, offer different explanations for why these racial patterns are unjust. The different theories will, however, begin from a basis of broad agreement that these and similar racial patterns are prima facie unjust.

Social and political philosophy needs to explain whether these apparent racial injustices are, in fact, unjust, or whether the apparent injustices are merely apparent, and not also real. In addition, assuming for the sake of argument that some of the obvious disparities between whites and nonwhites are the result of injustice, social and political philosophy needs to explain exactly what makes these disparities unjust. This is where we must begin in order to understand race-related injustice from a philosophical point of view.

1

One common explanation of the injustice of social and economic disparities between whites and nonwhites in the contemporary United States is linked to a causal claim about the origin of race-related injustice. It is plausible that much, perhaps most, race-related injustice that is suffered by nonwhites in the United States was originally caused by racist beliefs or attitudes on the part of whites toward nonwhites. For instance, educational disparities between whites and nonwhites in the United States presumably exist today at least in part because of whites' current or past beliefs that nonwhites do not deserve to receive the same education to which whites are entitled, possibly because whites thought that such education would be wasted on nonwhites. A similar causal explanation could be given to link nonwhites' disadvantages with respect to income, wealth, incarceration, education, health care, and so on, to beliefs and attitudes on the part of white Americans about what opportunities, resources, and treatment nonwhite Americans morally deserve.

Such racist beliefs and attitudes of individual white Americans are evidently morally objectionable. Some might therefore suggest that the reason why the patterns of racial disparity with respect to opportunities, resources, and treatment discussed above are unjust is that these patterns are caused by beliefs and attitudes on the part of whites toward nonwhites that are racist, and therefore morally objectionable. I will call the perspective that tries to understand race-related injustice on the basis of this suggestion the ethical perspective, because it takes interpersonal racism on the part of individuals to be primary and social patterns of racial disparity to be secondary with respect to both causation and explanation. The ethical perspective assumes both that interpersonal racism on the part of whites is the primary or sole cause of injustice related to race and that the causation of injustice related to race by interpersonal racism explains why injustice related to race in question is, in fact, unjust.

In contrast to the ethical perspective, we may define a social perspective on race-related injustice as a perspective that focuses on social systems and the institutions, groups, power relationships, and causal patterns that constitute them. The social perspective assigns a special role to concepts such as racial domination and oppression in its analysis of race-related injustices. Individuals' beliefs, desires, intentions, and actions may contribute to relations of racial domination or oppression, but racial domination and oppression are fundamentally relations between social groups, and not between particular individuals. Explanations of racial injustices from the social viewpoint will run primarily from causes at the level of social systems to effects at the level of individuals, rather than the other way around. The social perspective on race-related injustice need not deny the existence or significance of interpersonal racism, any more than the ethical perspective need deny the existence or significance of social relationships of domination or oppression between racial groups. The social perspective simply denies that interpersonal racism is prior to social patterns of racial injustice in order of causation or explanation, and maintains that the order of causation and explanation is, in fact, the reverse.

In the first section of this chapter, I will examine the case that is made in support of the ethical perspective on race-related injustice by J. L. A. Garcia in a series of articles on the nature of racism. I will argue that Garcia's account of the concept of racism is inadequate for several reasons, but chiefly because he assigns an implausibly great causal role to racism in the creation of race-related injustice. In the second section, I will examine Lawrence Blum's contrasting account of racism, arguing that Blum demonstrates a much clearer understanding of the explanatory limits of the concept of racism than Garcia does. In the third section, I will examine Charles W. Mills' conception of white supremacy, which he develops as part of his analysis of what he calls the racial contract. I will argue that Mills' conception of white supremacy can play a central role in an effort to understand race-related injustice from the social perspective, but that Mills' conception of white supremacy needs to be separated from his commitment to the philosophical methodology of social contractarianism in order to illuminate race-related injustice as fully as possible.

1. Garcia's Ethical Perspective on Racial Injustice

Garcia develops what he calls a volitional conception of racism in a series of four articles.[4] In three of the four articles, Garcia begins by criticizing the lack of clarity and precision with which the term "racism" is used not only in ordinary discourse, but even in philosophical circles.[5] He proposes to remedy this deficiency by articulating a conception of racism that meets eight well-defined criteria, of a sort that will be familiar to any reader of contemporary philosophy journals with an analytic bent. Garcia explicitly articulates these criteria only in his 1997 article, "Current Conceptions of Racism: A Critique of Some Recent Social Philosophy," but these criteria or some others quite similar to them tacitly guide Garcia's inquiry in the other three articles. Garcia states that an adequate conception of racism must:

(A) explain why racism is always immoral;

(B) allow for both interpersonal and institutional forms of racism, and explain how the two forms are connected to each other;

(C) allow practices, procedures, actions, beliefs, hopes, desires, fears, and goals to count as racist;

(D) include historical and imagined cases that intuitively count as racism, and exclude historical and imagined cases that intuitively do not;

(E) be internally consistent and free of undesirable implications;

(F) conform to everyday discourse about racism;

(G) remain consistent with past usage of the term "racism" or offer plausible reasons for transforming that usage; and

(H) have a structure that is similar to the concepts of anti-Semitism, homophobia, misogyny, and xenophobia.[6]

These methodological criteria for discovering an adequate conception of racism entail certain substantive assumptions about the nature of racism and our knowledge of racism. This should come as no surprise: methodological criteria always entail such assumptions, unless they are purely pragmatic in a sense of "pragmatic" that is very thin, indeed. Thus, to say that Garcia's methodological criteria entail substantive assumptions is not, so far, to criticize those criteria as inappropriate. But it is illuminating to examine some of the specific assumptions that Garcia's criteria do, in fact, entail:

(A) The wrongness of racism is primarily a moral, as opposed to a social or political, matter. That is, racism is primarily a moral vice of individual persons, and not primarily a political flaw of societies, institutions, or practices.

(B) Racism takes two forms, interpersonal and institutional, that are related to one another. Given criterion (A), one might reasonably expect Garcia to take interpersonal racism to be fundamental and institutional racism to be derivative from the former.

(C) Related to (B), both features of institutions, such as goals, practices, and procedures, and features of individuals, such as hopes, desires, and fears, can be racist. Nevertheless, given criterion (A), one might reasonably expect Garcia to take the former set of features to be derivative from the latter.

(D) Our intuitions (whoever "we" may be) are a reliable guide to what is and is not racist; also, it is equally important to account for historical examples and imaginary examples of racism.

(E) A conception of racism that avoids logical inconsistencies and undesirable (to whom?) implications is more likely to capture the nature of racism than one that does not.

(F) Everyday discourse about racism is a reliable guide to what racism is.

(G) Past usage of the term "racism" is a reliable guide to what racism is.

(H) Racism is similar in structure to anti-Semitism, homophobia, misogyny, and xenophobia. Garcia interprets all of the above as forms of antipathy, ill-will, or lack of consideration on the part of an individual moral agent toward members of a certain social group.

It is worth stopping to reflect a moment on some of these assumptions. Assumptions (D), (E), (F), and (G) suggest that Garcia understands himself to be engaged in a classically analytic philosophical project, namely, the tracing of the meaning of a term as it is used in ordinary language. This is not surprising, since he explicitly embraces analytic methodology in his 1999 article, "Philosophical Analysis and the Moral Concept of Racism." Since "racism" is not a term of art but a term that is widely used in both technical and everyday language, Garcia does not consider himself at liberty to stipulate its meaning. Instead, he is bound to place his trust primarily in the guidance of intuition and ordinary language to lead him to the reality of racism.

Assumptions (A), (B), (C), and (H) spell out some of the guidance that Garcia believes he gets from intuition and ordinary language. Both (B) and (C) suggest that racism takes two forms, interpersonal and institutional, which need to be accounted for and whose interrelationship needs to be explained. And both (A) and, in the final analysis, (H), suggest that according to intuition and ordinary language, interpersonal racism will take explanatory priority over institutional racism, so that the latter will need to be explained in terms of the former. Garcia's assumption (A), that racism is fundamentally a moral rather than a social or political matter, focuses his analysis on the individual moral agent, and not on the social institutions, structures, and practices that make up the context in which the agent acts. Likewise, his assumption (H), that racism is similar to anti-Semitism, homophobia, and misogyny insofar as it is fundamentally a matter of individual feeling rather than social structure, suggests that the features of social structures, institutions, and practices that Garcia identifies as reflecting institutional racism are to be explained in terms of their relation to individuals' beliefs, desires, intentions, and actions, rather than the other way around.

Once Garcia's methodological criteria have been carefully examined, the conception of racism that he ends up advocating is not much of a surprise. He maintains that "racism" has two senses. First, racism is "race-based disaffection for persons deemed to belong to a certain race." Second, and derivatively, racism is "a differential lack of goodwill such that one doesn't much care about people assigned to a certain racial group, precisely because they are deemed to belong to that group."[7] Both the disaffection and the differential lack of goodwill are conceived primarily as traits of individuals, and secondarily as influences upon the practices, procedures, actions, and goals of institutions. Since Garcia stipulates that institutional racism is the effects of interpersonal racism on social institutions, structures, and practices, institutional racism is explained as an effect of interpersonal racism. Institutional racism would not and could not exist had there never been individual racists who manifested interpersonal racism.[8]

Other philosophers of race have pointed out a number of flaws in Garcia's volitional conception of racism. Tommie Shelby questions Garcia's methodological assumption (A), which commits him to the view that every instance of racism is morally wrong. Shelby argues that this assumption stacks the deck in favor of Garcia's preferred volitional account of racism and against a more traditional doxastic account, which maintains that racist beliefs are a necessary component of racism.[9] After all, we do not normally hold people to be morally blameworthy simply on account of the beliefs that they hold, in the absence of feelings or actions that are based on the beliefs in question. Shelby points out that if we relax Garcia's assumption by maintaining not that every instance of racism is morally wrong, but only that every instance of racism is morally significant, then it is possible to understand racist beliefs as playing an important role in the constitution of racism.[10] Shelby goes on to argue that racist beliefs are a necessary constituent of racism, since a person's feeling antipathy or failing to feel appropriate goodwill toward members of a certain race cannot fairly be called racist unless we know what beliefs motivate this antipathy or lack of goodwill.[11] Moreover, Shelby argues that racist feelings are not a necessary component of racism because a person who believed that persons of a certain race were inferior and deserving of ill-treatment and who acted upon those beliefs without feeling any particular antipathy or lack of goodwill toward members of the race in question would surely be a racist in virtue of her beliefs, even in the absence of antipathy or lack of goodwill.[12]

Similarly, Charles W. Mills points out that Garcia's assumptions (F) and (H) are in significant tension with one another because (H) stipulates that racism is similar to other forms of hostility or enmity but not that it is similar to sexism. Yet (F) requires that any acceptable analysis of the concept of racism should conform to common usage of the term "racism," and racism is most commonly compared to sexism, which is not a form of hostility or enmity at all.[13] Mills also echoes Shelby in arguing that it is much more difficult than Garcia acknowledges to disentangle beliefs from volitions.[14] In particular, Mills argues that feelings of ill-will toward persons who happen to be of a certain race may be well-grounded or ill-grounded depending upon the epistemic status of the beliefs upon which the feelings are based. For this reason, the feelings cannot be evaluated separately from the beliefs.[15] The entanglement of feelings with beliefs becomes especially problematic for Garcia in considering the case of the benevolent, condescending racist. Since the benevolent, condescending racist does desire that members of a certain race receive what he believes to be good for them, his racism can be challenged only by evaluating the truth and the justification of his beliefs about what is good for members of the race in question.[16]

The criticisms raised by Shelby and Mills raise serious obstacles to the acceptance of Garcia's volitional account of racism as an adequate conception of racism. My main goal in the present chapter, however, is not to develop an adequate conception of racism, but to determine whether the ethical perspective or the social perspective sheds more light on race-related injustice. From the vantage point of this goal, a more serious problem with Garcia's conception of racism is the fact that it makes unsubstantiated causal claims about the relationship between interpersonal racism and institutional racism.

Garcia stipulates that institutional racism is the institutional effects of interpersonal racism.[17] He does not discuss the question whether there is any race-related injustice that does not amount to an instance of institutional racism, but he offers few clues about whether this is because he believes that no such race-related injustice exists or because any such injustice is simply beyond the scope of his inquiry. With respect to institutional racism, Garcia has little or nothing to say about the possibility of institutional racism subsisting in the absence of active, conscious, interpersonal racism on the part of individuals. Indeed, at one point, Garcia goes so far as to suggest that this possibility does not exist.

Consider the following example, taken from Garcia's 1999 article, "Philosophical Analysis and the Moral Concept of Racism." After articulating his volitional conception of racism and explaining the logical dependence of institutional racism on interpersonal racism, Garcia considers the question whether institutional racism can persist once interpersonal racism has been eradicated. Garcia asserts without argument that institutional racism can persist under such conditions, but only in a "rather marginal and insignificant" form.[18] Here Garcia makes the elementary mistake of presuming that an effect will practically vanish once its cause disappears. This, of course, does not follow, because whether an effect can persist only in the presence of its cause depends on the details of the causal relationship between the two. Garcia has not examined the causal relationship, as opposed to the logical relationship, between institutional and interpersonal racism at all carefully. All that he can establish on the basis of his conception of racism is that since institutional racism is defined as the institutional effects of interpersonal racism, the current existence of institutional racism logically entails the current or past existence of people who are or were interpersonal racists.[19]

This is more than a minor logical mistake. In claiming that institutional racism can barely exist without the current existence of interpersonal racism, Garcia forecloses the possibility that institutional racism might become strong enough at a certain point to go on generating advantages for some racial groups, such as whites, and disadvantages for others, such as nonwhites, without needing the active support of racist feelings against nonwhites on the part of whites. Indeed, as I shall discuss later in this chapter, Charles W. Mills argues in *The Racial Contract* that something very similar to this has, in fact, occurred in Western history.

For these reasons, the most serious problems with Garcia's account of racism from the vantage point of the present inquiry are that it offers us no help with exploring any form of race-related injustice that does not amount to institutional racism and that it makes the unjustified claim that eradicating interpersonal racism would automatically cause institutional racism to wither away. Since understanding and addressing the full scope of race-related injustice is a primary goal of this book, we cannot use Garcia's conception of racism as the focus of our inquiry.

2. Blum's Conception of Racism and Racial Injustice

Lawrence Blum develops a conception of racism that avoids some of the pitfalls of Garcia's conception in his recent book, *"I'm Not a Racist, But..."*: *The Moral Quandary of Race.*[20] Blum begins by distinguishing between racial antipathy and racial inferiorization. Racial antipathy, much like Garcia's interpersonal racism, is hostility toward a certain group that is viewed as racially defined. Racial inferiorization is treating a certain group as morally inferior to another group on the basis of a belief that the first group is inferior to the second by virtue of its biological nature.[21] Garcia, of course, would not count racial inferiorization as a form of racism unless it was accompanied by racial antipathy.

Next, Blum distinguishes between three forms of racism. Personal racism is attitudes, beliefs, acts, or behaviors on the part of individuals that are characterized or motivated by racial antipathy or racial inferiorization. Social racism is attitudes, beliefs, and stereotypes that are widely shared and expressed across a society that are characterized by racial antipathy or racial inferiorization. Finally, institutional racism is racial antipathy or racial inferiorization that is perpetuated by some social institution as a totality.[22] Again, each of these forms of racism is defined more expansively than Garcia would permit insofar as each form may involve racial inferiorization in the absence of racial antipathy.

Blum's key move from the point of view of the present inquiry is to draw an explicit distinction between institutional racism and racial injustice. Blum maintains that institutional racism contributes to many forms of racial injustice, but denies that the two phenomena are co-extensive. A form of racial injustice is caused by institutional racism if and only if the racially unjust practices that are part of the institution are shaped by either racial antipathy or racial inferiorization at the personal or social level. By way of illustrating the distinction between racial injustice and institutional racism, Blum offers the example of literacy tests for voting. Imagine that a legislative body established a literacy qualification for voting in a certain jurisdiction and that the literacy qualification was enforced by a fair literacy test. Blum maintains that if the literacy qualification were to disadvantage African-American voters disproportionately, then the literacy qualification would therefore be racially unjust. The literacy qualification would not, however, be a form of institutional racism unless the legislative body adopted the test specifically as a means of disadvantaging African-American voters disproportionately.[23] Blum sees racial justice as a matter of racially fair outcomes of actions, policies, and practices and institutional racism as a matter of racist motivations for actions, policies, and practices.

To determine whether Blum's conception of racism is the best conception available is beyond the scope of inquiry of this chapter. Blum's conception of racism demonstrates, however, that it is possible to develop a conception of racism that does not fall prey to some of the key pitfalls of Garcia's conception, such as Garcia's misguided attempt to isolate racist feelings from racist beliefs. More importantly, Blum's conception of racism demonstrates that it is possible to take seriously the moral wrongs of personal racism and the bad effects of personal racism on social institutions without claiming either that institutional racism would necessarily vanish if personal racism were eliminated or that all forms of racial injustice are caused by institutional racism. This last point is particularly noteworthy, since social and political philosophy should be concerned equally with all forms of racial injustice, whether or not they are causally linked to personal racism. Blum's conception of racism provides social and political philosophy with the conceptual space that it needs to understand and address racial injustice in general, without regard to its causal origin.

3. Mills' Conception of White Supremacy and Racial Injustice

Charles W. Mills takes a different approach to understanding race-related injustice in his recent work in the philosophy of race.[24] Rather than following Garcia's lead by beginning by identifying a concept that already has some currency in everyday and technical speech and then establishing some criteria by which to identify a workable version of this concept, Mills identifies a social phenomenon that he wants to understand and then seeks to fashion a concept that will illuminate this phenomenon. The phenomenon in question is white people's domination and oppression of nonwhite people around the world since the beginning of the age of European exploration. Mills seeks to conceptualize this system of racial domination as "global white supremacy," which he claims is "the unnamed political system that has made the modern world what it is today."[25] Later in the same passage, Mills continues,

> Ironically, the most important system of recent global history – the system of domination by which white people have historically ruled over and, in certain important ways, continue to rule over nonwhite people – is not seen as a political system at all. It is just taken for granted; it is the background against which

other systems, which we *are* to see as political, are highlighted. This book is an attempt to redirect your vision, to make you see what, in a sense, has been there all along.[26]

That is to say, Mills presents *The Racial Contract* as an extended argument for the conclusion that we ought to examine race-related injustice from the social viewpoint, focusing on relationships of racial domination and oppression rather than on individuals' beliefs, desires, feelings, and actions.

Mills borrows the term "white supremacy" from legal scholar Frances Lee Ansley, who defines it in the following way:

> [White supremacy is] a political, economic, and cultural system in which whites overwhelmingly control power and material resources, conscious and unconscious ideas of white superiority and entitlement are widespread, and relations of white dominance and non-white subordination are daily reenacted across a broad array of institutions, and social settings.[27]

In seeking to understand this system of domination, Mills is trying to inform political philosophy with a more accurate picture of how Western democracies have historically operated. Mills argues that the Western states that were purportedly founded on the egalitarian ideals of social contact theory have actually been based on hierarchical relations between the privileged persons who are members of the dominant white race and the disadvantaged subpersons who are members of various subordinate nonwhite races.[28] Tracing the contours of the political system of global white supremacy is made easier by the fact that moral and political philosophers explicitly described this system and sought to justify its operation for several centuries.[29] Mills himself traces the suppressed history of early modern philosophy of race in *The Racial Contract*. Also, in *Race and the Enlightenment*, Emmanuel Eze has revealed how such pillars of the Enlightenment as Hume, Kant, Jefferson, and Hegel all expressly endorse white supremacy, often arguing at great length for its justifiability.[30]

Such historical arguments might lead one to the conclusion that white supremacy used to be an important category of political analysis when white supremacy was enshrined in both positive laws and the political philosophy that justified those laws, but that this category is no longer so important for two reasons. First, the laws that enforced white supremacy have by and large been overturned, even in the last great bastions of white supremacy, the United States and South Africa. Second, political philosophers no longer expressly advocate global white supremacy. If this argument were sound, then the concept "white supremacy" might interest the political or social historian and the historian of ideas, but it would hardly merit the attention of a social and political philosopher.

Mills argues to the contrary that "white supremacy" remains a crucial concept for social and political philosophy for two reasons. First, race continues even now to shape our sense of who counts as a full-fledged person and who does not. As Mills takes pains to show, nonwhites are treated as counting for less than whites in the juridicial, political, economic, and cultural realms of life in the United States. The economic, cultural, aesthetic, and intellectual achievements of nonwhites are both denigrated and appropriated without acknowledgment by whites. In all of these areas, racial distinctions between white persons and nonwhite subpersons are alive and well in the United States, even four decades after the demise of Jim Crow.[31]

Second, for whites and nonwhites alike, race continues to be a source of differential entitlement to property and to respectful treatment by others.[32] Examples of differential entitlement along racial lines abound, but I will illustrate the truth of Mills' claim by examining just one example, namely, the racial disparities in income and wealth analyzed by Melvin Oliver and Thomas Shapiro in their award-winning study, *Black Wealth/White Wealth*.[33] Oliver and Shapiro show that while the income gap between white Americans and African-Americans is significant, the gap between the wealth of white Americans and that of African-Americans is simply staggering. Whereas the income of the median African-American household is 38% less than that of the median white American household, the median African-American household possesses net worth (total assets less total debts) that is 92% less than the net worth of the median white American household.[34] Worse, the median African-American family in practically any demographic category you care to examine possesses zero net financial assets (total assets less home equity less total debts).[35] These racial disparities in wealth were largely produced by economic discrimination against African-Americans on the part of the US government from the time of racial slavery up through the passage of federal civil rights legislation in the late 1960s.[36] The disparities persist and continue to grow today under the influence of economic factors that favor increases in wealth for those who already happen to possess significant wealth and decreases in wealth for those who do not happen to do so.[37] Failure to examine the continuing operation of white supremacy in such a context simply serves to entrench further the unjust advantages that whites have over nonwhites.[38]

Mills defines global white supremacy as "the European domination of the planet [both *de jure* and *de facto*] that has left us with the racialized distributions of economic, political, and cultural power that we have today."[39] Mills distinguishes sharply between white supremacy and what is usually called "racism." By "racism," people usually mean "a complex of ideas, values and attitudes," whereas "[w]*hite supremacy* and *global white supremacy*, in contrast, have the semantic virtues of clearly signaling reference to a system, a particular kind of polity, so structured as to advantage whites."[40]

In some contexts, and particularly in *The Racial Contract*, Mills seeks to explain white supremacy as the result of a racial contract. The racial contract is a counterpart of the social contract, which produces a racialized, hierarchical social order rather than a race-neutral, egalitarian social order. Whites create the racial contract by agreeing (1) to distinguish between whites, who are full moral persons, and nonwhites, who are moral subpersons; (2) to act on the basis of a *Herrenvolk* ethics that treats only white persons, and not nonwhite subpersons, as deserving of full moral concern and respect; and (3) to establish a racialized polity in which only white persons, and not nonwhite subpersons, may participate as full, equal members.[41] Once these three conditions are established in a society, white supremacy exists there; and when these conditions have been established around the world by European colonialism, global white supremacy exists.

Mills divides the history of white supremacy into three periods. In the founding period, European philosophers at the dawn of the Enlightenment transformed medieval Europe's expressly hierarchical distinction between Christians and heathens into another, expressly hierarchical distinction between white persons and nonwhite subpersons. One crucial difference between the earlier religious distinction and the later racial one was that a heathen could choose to become a Christian through conversion, but a nonwhite subperson could not become a white person through any voluntary process.[42] This was followed by the lengthy period of *de jure* global white supremacy, during which white peoples dominated and oppressed nonwhite peoples around the globe and accepted that this power relationship was justified by their moral, legal, cognitive, and aesthetic superiority to nonwhites.[43] Since the beginning of the end of European colonial rule of most of the rest of the world around 1945, Mills argues that we have lived in a period of *de facto* global white supremacy. Whites still exercise the vast majority of political, legal, economic, and cultural power, yet it is considered bad form to discuss or analyze this continued pattern of white domination over nonwhites because this domination is not officially considered to exist or to be justified morally. As a result, one can analyze, criticize, or organize against *de facto* white supremacy only at the risk of being charged with being a racist oneself.[44]

Mills sees the political system of global white supremacy as closely related to individuals' racist beliefs, desires, feelings, and behaviors, but he insists on the importance of treating the political system as cause and the individuals' beliefs, desires, feelings, and behaviors as effect. Speaking about black-Jewish relations in an essay entitled, "Dark Ontologies," Mills writes,

> If we see these problems solely in term of individual prejudice and bigotry, free-floating attitudes and cultural predispositions, we will miss crucial realities that need to be incorporated into an adequate explanation. In other words, we need to talk about race itself as a political system, and the differential and evolving relations of blacks and Jews to it.[45]

Later on in the same essay, Mills expands upon this theme: "Appeals to moral toleration of difference will do no good if the system [of racial privilege] remains intact, because no matter how subjectively sincere people's intentions, the objective structure keeps recoalescing the [racial] identities in their old, antagonistic forms."[46]

Thus, Mills sees the political system of global white supremacy as the cause of beliefs, desires, feelings, and behaviors of individuals that the ethical perspective on racial justice would identify as racist. These subjective elements are, indeed, some of the more pernicious effects of the existence of global white supremacy. They are not, however, the key social reality that Mills is trying to understand. He is primarily interested instead in the political, social, economic, and cultural advantages that whites gain and nonwhites miss out on as a result of global white supremacy. These advantages can and do exist even if no one seeks to create them from motivations that Blum or Garcia would identify as racist. As Mills points out, the persistence of these advantages can even be ensured by cultural forces that discourage people from allowing themselves to become aware of these advantages.[47]

Mills' distinction between global white supremacy and racism allows him to maintain that not everyone who benefits from the existence of global white supremacy is a racist. Indeed, Mills argues that in a white supremacist polity, whites can be broken down into three categories:

(1) beneficiaries of the racial contract who are also signatories to it, that is, who endorse its operation;

(2) beneficiaries of the racial contract who are not also signatories to it, that is, who do not endorse its operation; and

(3) beneficiaries of the racial contract who not only avoid being signatories to the racial contract, but who also act as race traitors by working to undermine its operation.[48]

In making this distinction, Mills acknowledges the importance of the subjective, individual elements of interpersonally racist feelings, attitudes, beliefs, and behaviors that are the focus of the ethical perspective. After all, Mills' distinction between beneficiaries of the contract who are signatories to it and those who are not would be a distinction without a difference if people's beliefs, attitudes, and feelings toward the racial contract were irrelevant from a moral point of view. Nevertheless, Mills' conceptual focus always remains squarely upon white supremacy as a political system that generates social, political, economic, and cultural advantages for whites and corresponding disadvantages for nonwhites, rather than upon the elements of individual psychology on which the ethical perspective focuses.

Mills employs contractarian methodology not only descriptively, in order to explain how white supremacy actually did arise from agreements among white men to treat one another as morally equal persons and to treat nonwhites as morally inferior subpersons, but also normatively, in order to explain how whites and nonwhites ought to treat one another as morally equal persons who have equal rights to participate in establishing the political order and equal responsibilities to obey it.[49] He is therefore committed to arguing that a cleaned-up, nonwhite supremacist social contract would guarantee the emancipation of nonwhites from the forces of domination and oppression to which they have long been subjected.

Normative social contract theory has, however, long been subject to intense critique by political philosophers of a variety of stripes. In one of the best articulations of such a critique, Carole Pateman argues that while social contract theory purports to be a means of freeing people from any social and political authority that they have not freely consented to obey, it is in fact a means of permitting and encouraging people to subordinate themselves to all manner of forms of social, political, and economic domination.[50]

While a full evaluation of Mills' arguments for and Pateman's arguments against social contractarian methodology is beyond the scope of this chapter, it is worth noting that there are good reasons to be concerned about whether social contractarianism is the best available means for emancipating nonwhites from white supremacy. Fortunately, it is possible to separate Mills' concept of white supremacy, which is useful for understanding the social phenomenon on which the present book focuses, from Mills' commitment to normative social contract theory, which is at best a questionable means for emancipating nonwhites from white supremacy. The remainder of my argument will make regular use of the concept of white supremacy without presuming that Mills is correct to think that normative social contract theory provides the best prescription to address the problems of racial injustice that are caused by white supremacy.

Notes

1. Thomas M. Shapiro, *The Hidden Cost of Being African American: How Wealth Perpetuates Inequality* (New York: Oxford University Press, 2004), 38–39.
2. Henry Louis Gates, Jr., "Parable of the Talents," in Henry Louis Gates, Jr., and Cornel West, *The Future of the Race* (New York: Alfred A. Knopf, 1996), 24–25.
3. Linda H. Aiken and Douglas M. Sloane, "Quality of In-Patient AIDS Care: Does Race Matter?", in *Problem of the Century: Racial Stratification in the United States*, ed. Elijah Anderson and Douglas S. Massey (New York: Russell Sage Foundation, 2001), 247.
4. See J. L. A. Garcia, "The Heart of Racism," *Journal of Social Philosophy*, vol. 27, no. 1 (Spring 1996), 5–45; Garcia, "Current Conceptions of Racism: A Critique of Some Recent Social Philosophy," *Journal of Social Philosophy*, vol. 28, no. 2 (Fall 1997), 5–42; Garcia, "Philosophical Analysis and the Moral Concept of Racism," *Philosophy & Social Criticism*, vol. 25, no. 5 (1999), 1–32; and Garcia, "Racism and Racial Discourse," *The Philosophical Forum*, vol. 32, no. 2 (Summer 2001), 125–45.
5. Garcia, "The Heart of Racism," 5–6; "Current Conceptions of Racism," 5–7; and "Philosophical Analysis," 1–2.
6. Garcia, "Current Conceptions of Racism," 6–7.
7. Garcia, "Current Conceptions of Racism," 29.
8. Garcia, "Current Conceptions of Racism," 26.
9. Tommie Shelby, "Is Racism in the Heart?", *Journal of Social Philosophy* 33 (2002), 411–13.
10. Shelby, "Is Racism in the Heart?", 413–15.
11. Shelby, "Is Racism in the Heart?", 415–17.
12. Shelby, "Is Racism in the Heart?", 417–19.
13. Charles W. Mills, "'Heart Attack': A Critique of Jorge Garcia's Volitional Account of Racism," *Journal of Ethics* 7 (2003), 32–34.
14. Mills, "'Heart' Attack," 37–41.
15. Mills, "'Heart' Attack," 41–44.
16. Mills, "'Heart' Attack," 51–57.
17. Garcia, "Current Conceptions of Racism," 26.
18. Garcia, "Philosophical Analysis," 17.
19. Garcia, "Current Conceptions of Racism," 26.
20. Lawrence Blum, *"I'm Not a Racist, But...": The Moral Quandary of Race* (Ithaca: Cornell University Press, 2002).
21. Blum, *"I'm Not a Racist, But..."*, 8–9.

22. Blum, *"I'm Not a Racist, But..."*, 9.

23. Blum, *"I'm Not a Racist, But..."*, 22–26.

24. See Mills, *The Racial Contract* (Ithaca: Cornell University Press, 1997); *Blackness Visible: Essays on Philosophy and Race* (Ithaca: Cornell University Press, 1998); *From Class to Race: Essays in White Marxism and Black Radicalism* (Lanham, Md.: Rowman & Littlefield, 2003).

25. Mills, *Racial Contract*, 1.

26. Mills, *Racial Contract*, 1–2; emphasis original.

27. Frances Lee Ansley, "Stirring the Ashes: Race, Class, and the Future of Civil Rights Scholarship," *Cornell Law Review* 74, no. 6 (Sept. 1989), 1024 n.

28. Mills, *Racial Contract*, 121–22.

29. Mills, *Blackness Visible*, 123.

30. Mills, *Racial Contract*, 19–31; Emmanuel Eze, ed., *Race and the Enlightenment: A Reader* (Cambridge, Mass.: Blackwell, 1997).

31. Mills, *From Class to Race*, 186–93.

32. Mills, *Blackness Visible*, 134–35.

33. Melvin L. Oliver & Thomas M. Shapiro, *Black Wealth/White Wealth: A New Perspective on Racial Inequality* (New York: Routledge, 1995).

34. Oliver & Shapiro, *Black Wealth/White Wealth*, 86.

35. Oliver & Shapiro, *Black Wealth/White Wealth*, 97.

36. Oliver & Shapiro, *Black Wealth/White Wealth*, 11–23.

37. Oliver & Shapiro, *Black Wealth/White Wealth*, 23–32.

38. Mills, *Blackness Visible*, 135–37.

39. Mills, *Blackness Visible*, 98.

40. Mills, *Blackness Visible*, 100; emphasis original.

41. Mills, *Racial Contract*, 109–11.

42. Mills, *Racial Contract*, 19–23.

43. Mills, *Racial Contract*, 23–30, 53–62.

44. Mills, *Racial Contract*, 30–31.

45. Mills, *Blackness Visible*, 74.

46. Mills, *Blackness Visible*, 93.

47. Mills, *Racial Contract*, 92–96.

48. Mills, *Racial Contract*, 11.

49. Mills, *From Class to Race*, 245–46.

50. Carole Pateman, *The Sexual Contract* (Stanford: Stanford University Press, 1988), 146.

Chapter Two
Police Violence and
the White Supremacist State

In chapter one, I argued for the general conclusion that the concept of white supremacy does a better job of explaining race-related injustice than the concept of racism. Abstract arguments for general conclusions may compel a reader's consent, but the reader's conviction may not follow unless a concrete, specific illustration of the force of the conclusion is supplied. This chapter is intended to supply such an illustration of the relative explanatory power of the concepts of white supremacy and racism. It is intended to illustrate the limits of the power of the concept of racism to explain one specific case of race-related injustice, and the superior power of the concept of white supremacy to explain the same case.

My argument for the superior explanatory power of the concept of white supremacy will focus on the light that this concept sheds on the history of police violence against African-American men in my hometown of Omaha, Nebraska. I hope that my detailed, concrete illustration of the application of the concept of white supremacy will convince the reader of its explanatory power. Social and political philosophy needs to be able to demonstrate the explanatory power of its concepts in such specific local contexts in order to prove itself relevant and useful to the struggle for racial justice in a white-dominated world.

I choose to focus specifically on the context of Omaha not only because I know it well, but also because the local racial politics of it are likely to resemble those of many cities in the midwestern and northeastern United States. Omaha was founded in 1854 and has had a significant nonwhite population since the Great Migration of African-Americans from the southern United States began in the 1910s.[1] Subsequently, African-Americans and white Americans have a long and frequently ugly history of relations with one another that now spans nine decades in Omaha. This history includes a wide range of forms of discrimination in education, housing, and employment against African-Americans by whites that has led to Omaha having a rate of poverty among African-Americans that is significantly higher than the 25% rate of African-American poverty for the United States as a whole.[2] It also includes a long history of hate crimes by whites against African-Americans, most notably the lynching of William Brown in 1919.[3] In short, race relations in Omaha are worth examining because they provide pointed examples of forms of racial injustice that are found to one degree or another in most cities in the United States.

The specific cases of race-related injustice on which I will focus in this chapter relate to Marvin Ammons and George Bibins, two African-American men killed by police officers in my hometown of Omaha, Nebraska, during the past fifteen years. I do not choose to examine the killings of Ammons and Bibins because they are more obviously unjust than other killings of other African-American men by police officers in other US cities. On the contrary, I examine these killings precisely because of their similarities to other such killings, which are sadly commonplace in the US. I also choose to examine the Ammons and Bibins killings because I am familiar with them, and because the fact that they took place in Omaha means that it is far less likely that they will ever attract the national notice that cases of police violence against African-Americans in New York and Los Angeles have attracted.

Consider, for instance, the extensive consideration that critical race theorists and others have devoted to the beating of Rodney King by officers of the Los Angeles Police Department and the riots that followed in the aftermath of the officers' acquittal on all charges in 1992.[4] While there is no denying the powerful effect that the police assault on Rodney King had on awareness of and debate about police violence against African-Americans, the intense focus of attention on this one case by theorists and the mass media alike may mislead some to think that such events occur exclusively or primarily in the largest urban centers in the US, such as Los Angeles and New York. The present chapter is, in part, an effort to correct that false impression.

I will begin by sketching the history of police violence against African-Americans in Omaha and then examining the details of the killings of Ammons and Bibins against the backdrop of this history in section one. In section two, I will examine how liberal political philosophy can identify the forms of injustice that are manifest in the killings of Ammons and Bibins. In section three, I will compare the diagnoses of the causes of the injustices that occurred in the Ammons and Bibins cases that could be offered from the ethical viewpoint and from the social viewpoint, and will argue that the diagnosis that could be offered from the social perspective is superior. I will conclude by considering whether the diagnosis offered from the social perspective is compatible with the theoretical framework of liberal political philosophy in section four.

1. The Police Shootings of Marvin Ammons and George Bibins

Between 1981 and 2000, officers of the Omaha Police Department shot and killed 18 persons in a city with a population of about 390,000. This figure is a little below the national per capita average. All of these persons have been male, and the overwhelming majority of them have been African-American. Although a majority of these men have exchanged gunfire with the police prior to being shot and several have been shot after leading police on a chase, very few of them were shot during or immediately after the commission of a crime. In several cases, witnesses have been unable to determine why the shooting victims fled from the police or began shooting at the police. Several of the victims have been unarmed. One might suspect that the victims have reacted fearfully to being approached by police, and that the victims' fearful reactions precipitated their being killed.[5]

A review of police killings of African-Americans in Omaha suggests that African-Americans would reasonably fear coming to harm at the hands of the police. Two historical examples are etched particularly deeply in the memories of long-time Omaha residents. On March 5, 1968, Alabama Governor George Wallace made his first presidential campaign appearance outside Alabama at Omaha's Civic Auditorium. After Wallace supporters attacked and beat anti-Wallace demonstrators, the demonstrators spilled out of the auditorium and began a night of rioting and looting on North 24th Street, the main commercial district of the predominately African-American near north side.[6] During the riot, a sixteen-year-old African-American boy named Howard Stevenson jumped through a pawn shop window. Off-duty police officer James F. Abbott, who was guarding the store, shot and killed Stevenson without warning. Abbott later claimed that Stevenson was stealing from the store when Abbott shot him, but other witnesses denied this. The Douglas County Attorney declined to charge Abbott with any crime, but commented that he would have filed burglary charges against Stevenson had he lived.[7]

A little over a year later, on June 24, 1969, Officer James L. Loder responded to a prowling call at a housing project in Omaha's predominately African-American near north side. Upon Loder's approach, a group of children, including a fourteen-year-old African-American girl named Vivian Strong, fled. Loder shot Strong once in the back, killing her. The five days of rioting that ensued resulted in 21 arrests, 88 injuries, and $750,000 in property damage to North 24th Street, damage which has never fully been repaired. The county attorney filed criminal charges against Loder, but Loder was acquitted on all counts.[8]

The killings of Stevenson and Strong by Abbott and Loder cemented in the minds of many African-American citizens of Omaha the impression that white police officers could and would kill African-Americans with impunity. This impression remains fresh today, as a result of two more recent, controversial killings by police officers.

On October 26, 1997, officer trainee Todd Sears and his partner stopped their cruiser to investigate an auto accident. Sears called Marvin Ammons, a 33-year-old African-American male, over to the cruiser to ask whether he had been involved in the accident. As Ammons leaned over to speak to Sears, Ammons' coat swung open to reveal a holstered handgun tucked into the waist of Ammons' pants. What ensued is not clear, but something apparently made Sears believe that Ammons was reaching for his gun. Sears fired his sidearm three times, hitting Ammons twice and killing him.[9] Officers sent to investigate the shooting found Ammons' gun, still in its holster, lying near Ammons' right hand. They also later discovered Ammons' cell phone in the police cruiser;

Sears and his partner could not account for its presence. Confusion about Sears' shooting of Ammons persists because the testimonies of the two officers present conflicted with each other, the testimony of other eyewitnesses, and the physical evidence.[10] Moreover, the video camera placed in every Omaha police cruiser to record such events could not help dispel the confusion because Sears' partner turned it off before Ammons approached the cruiser.[11]

In the hours and days following Sears' killing of Ammons, both the mayor and the president of the police union offered accounts of the killing that were intended to place Sears in a favorable light and that later turned out to be misleading or simply false.[12] The Police Department fueled suspicion that Sears' shooting of Ammons had been unjustified by declining to release information about the case either to the public or to Ammons' family. Ollie Reaves, Ammons' mother, eventually sued the City of Omaha for the right to see the evidence related to her son's death in order to determine whether there were grounds for a civil suit against either Sears or the City. The court ordered the City to allow Reaves and her lawyers to review the evidence, but the City appealed the decision to the Nebraska Supreme Court, claiming that it wished to avoid tainting the grand jury investigation into the killing. After the Supreme Court unanimously rejected the City's appeal, a county judge sent the sheriff to police headquarters to seize the documents and to arrest anyone, including the police chief, who tried to interfere.[13]

On January 26, 1998, a grand jury indicted Todd Sears on a charge of manslaughter in the shooting of Marvin Ammons.[14] Before Sears' trial, the court took the unusual step of permitting Sears' attorney to review the transcript of the grand jury deliberations.[15] On the basis of this review, Sears' attorney successfully moved to have the manslaughter charge dismissed on the grounds that one of the three alternate jurors, who was one of the three African-Americans among the sixteen jurors and three alternates, had taken too active a role in the deliberations.[16] The alternate juror later told reporters that she had been instructed by the special prosecutor that she could ask questions while evidence was presented, and she acted on that instruction.[17] On January 20, 1999, a second grand jury declined to indict Sears on any charge. This time, the special prosecutor refused to disclose the racial makeup of the grand jury, leading many to conclude that it was all white.[18] Ollie Reaves subsequently brought a wrongful death civil suit against Sears.[19] Despite the manifest failure of the defense to reconcile conflicts between the testimony of Sears, the testimony of other witnesses, and the physical evidence, the jury took only 90 minutes to decide that Sears had not used excessive deadly force and had not engaged his weapon without probable cause.[20]

Nearly three years after Sears killed Ammons, police-community tensions flared again when Officer Jerad Kruse shot and killed George Bibins, a 35-year-old African-American man. In the early morning of July 19, 2000, Kruse and his partner tried to pull Bibins over for a traffic violation. Bibins led the police on a high-speed chase for seven minutes, which ended when Bibins crashed the stolen vehicle he was driving into a utility pole.[21] Kruse approached the passenger side of the vehicle and shot Bibins once through the passenger window, killing him. Bibins was unarmed, although a screwdriver was found on the floor of his vehicle. After police officials interrogated Kruse, the chief of police took the unusual step of stating publicly, "We can't put our finger on [Kruse's] justification [for shooting Bibins]." The chief referred the shooting to both a grand jury and the county attorney.[22]

Initially, the county attorney charged Kruse with manslaughter in the Bibins killing.[23] The district court later suspended this charge in order to avoid compromising a grand jury investigation mandated by state law.[24] A grand jury of sixteen jurors and three alternates, including three African-Americans, was impaneled, and declined to indict Kruse on any criminal charge in the Bibins shooting, without offering an explanation for its decision.[25] The county attorney requested access to the records of the grand jury's deliberation to determine whether the grand jury had received some publicly unavailable evidence that exculpated Kruse.[26] The district court denied the County attorney access to the records in October 2000, and the Nebraska Supreme Court upheld that decision on appeal in May 2002. Both courts emphasized, however, that the County attorney was free to charge and prosecute Kruse without reviewing the grand jury records.[27] Despite these assurances from the courts and despite earlier having filed a charge of manslaughter against Kruse before any evidence had been presented to the grand jury, the county attorney decided in May 2002 not to file any criminal charges against Kruse.[28]

By this time, the Police Department had permitted Kruse to retire from the department on a disability pension based on post-traumatic stress disorder linked to his killing of Bibins. The committee vote split along racial lines, with four whites voting to permit Kruse to retire and two African-Americans voting not to permit him to do so.[29] As a result of his retirement, Kruse was under no obligation to cooperate with the police department's internal affairs investigation into his killing of Bibins, and he chose not to cooperate. As the police chief said in releasing the inconclusive results of the internal affairs investigation, "There are only two people who know truly what happened. One of them can't talk to us, and one of them won't." [30]

2. Liberal Political Philosophy and the Ammons and Bibins Killings

It is easy to see that a fair number of injustices occurred in the killings of Marvin Ammons and George Bibins, but it is important to articulate exactly what those injustices are. An accurate identification of the wrongs that were done in these cases is the only possible basis on which to diagnose the causes of the wrongs and to prescribe remedies for them. In order to begin to identify the symptoms of injustice, I will work within the theoretical framework that has dominated Western political philosophy since the beginning of the modern era, namely, liberal political philosophy. The core commitment of liberal political philosophy is to the idea that all persons are entitled to a full and equal complement of civil and political rights. Among the basic civil rights of all citizens are the rights to life, liberty, and security of the person. Among the basic political rights are the right to equality before the law and the right to be treated with equal respect by the state and its agents. From the viewpoint of liberal political philosophy, then, at least three kinds of injustice occurred in the Ammons and Bibins cases.

(1) My extensive research into six years' worth of newspaper coverage of the Ammons and Bibins killings leads me to conclude that neither killing was justified. This conclusion is, of course, debatable, because the secrecy of grand jury proceedings entails that not all the evidence about either killing is publicly available. Nevertheless, the evidence that is publicly available in each case strongly suggests that Officers Sears and Kruse each responded hastily and excessively when they encountered Ammons and Bibins, respectively. On this ground, a liberal theory of justice would conclude that Sears and Kruse unjustifiably deprived Ammons and Bibins, respectively, of their rights to security of their persons, liberty, and life. The fundamental nature of each of these rights is evidence of the seriousness of these offenses.

(2) The judicial system failed to hold Sears responsible for killing Ammons and to hold Kruse responsible for killing Bibins. Of three predominately white grand juries that deliberated about the two killings, only one managed to return an indictment. In that case, namely, the first grand jury that examined Sears' killing of Ammons, the trial judge and Sears' defense attorney found a way to get the indictment dismissed. In the Bibins case, the county attorney declined to file charges against Kruse again after the grand jury failed to return an indictment, even though he had brought charges against Kruse before the grand jury convened and even though the courts reassured him that he was free to bring charges again. The president of the Omaha chapter of the NAACP spoke for many when he concluded, "There is not much thought of a white person getting a guilty verdict in a crime involving a black person. I'd say if Marvin Ammons had been the son of a wealthy white person in west Omaha, it would be a different story. I'd say the officer would be looking for a different job."[31] From the viewpoint of liberal political philosophy, the courts failed to treat Sears and Kruse, on the one hand, and Ammons and Bibins, on the other, as equals before the law. Sears and Kruse did not have to answer to the courts for killing Ammons and Bibins because the life of a white police officer counts for more than the life of an African-American citizen in Omaha, Nebraska, just as it does in many other US jurisdictions.

(3) Whereas the first two forms of injustice were done by the state or its officers to the shooting victims themselves, the third form of injustice was done by the state to the African-American community in Omaha. One way in which a liberal state respects the political rights of its citizens is by making itself accountable equally to all of its citizens. Throughout the Ammons and Bibins cases, the police department, the mayor, the county attorney, and the county courts repeatedly showed that they did not see themselves as being accountable to Omaha's African-American citizens. After watching white police officers killing African-American men with impunity for decades, African-American citizens of Omaha

justifiably feared that Sears and Kruse had killed Ammons and Bibins, respectively, without justification. They justifiably believed that the police and the mayor had conspired to cover up the unjustified killing of Ammons. And they justifiably believed that the courts' failure to bring either Sears or Kruse to trial on criminal charges was the result of a lack of concern by the courts for the lives of African-Americans.

African-American citizens of Omaha were justified in desiring (1) that their government make every effort to determine how and why Sears and Kruse killed Ammons and Bibins, respectively, (2) that their government make a full and accurate account of the killings public, and (3) that their government hold the officers criminally accountable for the killings. Their government failed them on all three counts. Thus, on the view of liberal political philosophy, their government failed to uphold the basic political rights of African-American citizens of Omaha and failed to show them the equal respect that is their due.

These three forms of injustice together make up the liberal identification of what was wrong with the local government's handling of the Ammons and Bibins shootings. Liberal political philosophy has much to say here because it has a well-developed, finely articulated catalogue of civil and political rights and liberties to appeal to in identifying injustice, and the excessive, unjustified use of force by a police officer against a citizen is a paradigm case of injustice for liberal political theory. It is not quite so obvious, however, how liberal political philosophy will diagnose the causes of the injustices that it has identified in the Ammons and Bibins cases. What liberal political philosophy says about these two issues will largely depend on the viewpoint from which liberals seek to diagnose and remedy the causes of the injustices.

3. Ethical and Social Perspectives on Police Violence

As I said in chapter one, liberal political philosophy could seek the causes of race-related injustice from either the ethical viewpoint or the social viewpoint. The ethical viewpoint looks for causes of injustice at the level of individual beliefs, desires, feelings, and actions, and conceptualizes the causes that it finds at this level as forms of racism. The social viewpoint, by contrast, looks for causes of injustice at the level of social systems and the institutions, groups, power relationships, and causal patterns that constitute them, and conceptualizes the causes that it finds at this level as forms of white supremacy. In this section of the chapter, I will examine the factors that each of these viewpoints might diagnose as the causes of the injustices that we have observed in the Ammons and Bibins killings.

If we look for causes from the ethical viewpoint, the logical first step is to try to identify individuals who contributed causally to the injustices done in the Ammons and Bibins cases who harbored racist beliefs, desires, or feelings that might have caused them to perform racist acts. Our search would presumably begin with Sears and Kruse themselves, and then spread out to include other police officers, police union officials, the mayor, the county attorney, grand jury members, and possibly other officers of the court. Unfortunately, this search quickly runs into a couple of significant roadblocks.

First, there is little direct evidence that individuals who causally contributed to the injustices done in the Ammons and Bibins cases did, in fact, harbor racist beliefs, desires, or feelings. At most, one can find hints of irrational fears about African-American men in isolated remarks made by Todd Sears and Jerad Kruse shortly after they shot Marvin Ammons and George Bibins, respectively.[32] I doubt that these remarks are sufficient to construct a satisfactory account of the causes of Sears and Kruse unjustly killing Ammons and Bibins, respectively. But even if they are sufficient for this purpose, they are certainly not a sufficient basis for constructing a satisfactory account of the injustices done to Ammons and Bibins by failing to treat them as full, equal citizens before the law and to the African-American citizens of Omaha by failing to treat them with the equal respect that is due to all citizens. The reason for this is that if individuals were responsible for these injustices, the individuals concerned were not Todd Sears and Jerad Kruse but other public officials such as the mayor, police union officials, the county attorney, and other officers of the courts. One can speculate about whether these individuals harbor racist beliefs, desires, and feelings, but I can find no direct evidence that they do.

Second, the search for causes of injustice at the level of individual beliefs, desires, feelings, and actions misleads us by encouraging us to see the Ammons and Bibins killings as surprising. It encourages us to view the killings as anomalies that stand out against a broad background of actions with non-racist motivations. The injustices done in Sears' killing of Ammons, Kruse's killing of Bibins, and all the other white police officers' killings of African-American men over the past four decades of Omaha history are understood from the ethical viewpoint as singular phenomena that can be completely explained by unique, idiosyncratic causes located in the minds of the individual agents. These idiosyncratic psychological causes of racist acts are viewed, in turn, as anomalous deviations from normal, non-racist psychology. From the ethical viewpoint, then, the stories of Marvin Ammons and George Bibins are just one isolated racist act after another, one anomaly after another, one surprise after another.

The police killings of Ammons and Bibins and the government's response to the killings may have been a lot of things, but they were not surprising. As a member of the first grand jury in the Sears case said in response to the second grand jury's failure to indict Sears, "The shock would have come had they returned an indictment. It's a bunch of bunk. The whole system is. And they wonder how black people can be so angry."[33] The main problem with the ethical viewpoint lies in its individualistic diagnosis of the causes of the injustices that are manifest in the killings of Ammons and Bibins. The race-related injustice that is manifest in police killings in Omaha is not a racist anomaly within a race-neutral system, but an expression of what is at the heart of the system itself.[34]

From the social viewpoint, by contrast, the killings of Ammons and Bibins do not appear as surprising malfunctions within an otherwise harmoniously functioning liberal democracy, but as the ordinary functioning of a *de facto* white supremacist state. In such a state, all adults are explicitly said to be full and equal citizens, but tacitly, only whites are really treated as full and equal citizens, while nonwhites are systematically treated as inferior and properly subordinate.[35] Two chief aims of a *de facto* white supremacist state are (1) to create, reinforce, and perpetuate white supremacy over non-whites and (2) to prevent people from talking about or even noticing that this is going on. Under the rule of such a state, both expressly justifying white supremacy by appeal to the moral superiority of whites over nonwhites and doing anything effectively to undermine this supremacy in fact are viewed as wrong.[36]

It would not be correct to classify the local government of Omaha as currently being a *de jure* white supremacist state. It is now more than thirty years since Omaha ceased to use the force of law overtly to segregate its schools, its neighborhoods, its public accommodations, and its workforce by race.[37] But despite the end of *de jure* segregation in Omaha a generation ago, the local government continues to act in ways that effectively support white supremacy in all of these spheres of public life. The killings of Ammons and Bibins clearly demonstrate that the local government of Omaha continues to be of, by, and for white Omahans, as it has been for a century and a half. As the president of an African-American business association in Omaha said when the second grand jury failed to indict Sears, "The Police Department's job is to enforce law and order for the white community. They take care of their own."[38] This is the ostensive definition of a white supremacist state.

The diagnosis of the causes of the injustices that are manifest in the police killings of Ammons and Bibins from the social viewpoint is superior to the diagnosis from the ethical viewpoint in two key respects. (1) Whereas the ethical viewpoint can provide little direct evidence to show that key individual players in the Ammons and Bibins cases harbored racist beliefs, desires, and feelings, the social viewpoint can provide plenty of direct evidence to show that the local government of Omaha and its agencies functioned to serve the interests of whites at the expense of non-whites by treating whites as full and equal citizens and nonwhites as less than full and equal citizens. (2) Whereas the ethical viewpoint views the police killings of Ammons and Bibins and the injustices that followed them as anomalous and surprising deviations from normal, non-racist behavior and as springing from unique, isolated, idiosyncratic psychological causes, the social viewpoint connects the many individual cases of police killings of African-American men in Omaha (and in other US cities) over the past several decades into one systematic picture that reveals the patterns and similarities that connect them.

Despite these advantages, the diagnosis of the causes of the injustices in the Ammons and Bibins cases from the social viewpoint is open to an important objection from the ethical viewpoint. A critic might say that it is one thing to identify a pattern of injustices, as the social viewpoint clearly does; but it is quite another to explain how and why these injustices arise from human agents and their actions. Whatever its other defects, the ethical viewpoint's diagnosis at least connects the injustices that appear in the Ammons and Bibins cases, on the one hand, to particular human agents and their actions and motivations for action, on the other. From the ethical viewpoint, it may not be obvious that the social viewpoint offers a causal explanation of the injustices, as opposed to an observation of certain patterns or regularities that connect a certain set of phenomena.

As the history of the development of white supremacy from *de jure* to *de facto* makes clear, however, existing *de facto* white supremacy is linked to individuals' actions and motivations for action. The links just are not as simple and direct as the diagnosis from the ethical viewpoint makes them out to be. The current *de facto* white supremacist local government of Omaha, Nebraska, developed out of the *de jure* white supremacist local government that existed prior to the 1960s. In this earlier period of the history of white supremacy in Omaha, white citizens of Omaha generally believed and said they believed that whites were superior to non-whites and that non-whites ought to be subordinate to whites. These beliefs informed and motivated many of their actions, including those that directly affected the constitution and operation of local government.

After a painful transition period in the 1960s, *de facto* white supremacy replaced its *de jure* forerunner in the 1970s. Since then, whites have continued to dominate non-whites, and the social structures that sustain and enforce that domination have their causal roots in the earlier, *de jure* period of white supremacy. The causal forces that sustain the patterns of white supremacy are now located in social structures and political institutions that were designed in the earlier period but continue to function now. In this way, the social viewpoint connects current racial injustices to past racist beliefs, desires, and feelings through currently existing structures and institutions. Both social systems and individual actions play a role in the causal story about the origin of current injustices that is told from the social viewpoint.

4. Liberal Political Philosophy and the Social Perspective on Racial Injustice

In section three, I argued that the diagnosis of the causes of the injustices that are manifest in the police killings of Ammons and Bibins from the social viewpoint is superior to the diagnosis from the ethical viewpoint in two key respects and that the diagnosis from the social viewpoint can be defended against an important objection from the ethical viewpoint. In this final section of the chapter, I will consider whether the diagnosis of the causes of the injustices from the social viewpoint is compatible with the theoretical framework that was used to identify the injustices, namely, liberal political philosophy.

There can be no doubt that liberal political philosophy is in tension with the social viewpoint. Liberalism focuses on the rights, freedoms, responsibilities, and well-being of individuals, whereas the social perspective focuses on social systems and the institutions, groups, power relationships, and causal patterns that make them up. Moreover, liberalism's chief goal is to protect the freedom and well-being of individuals against a variety of threats. Liberalism traditionally views the power relationships between social institutions and social groups, on the one hand, and individuals, on the other, as chief among the threats to individual rights and freedoms. Thus, liberalism not only has a different focus from the social perspective, it also tends to view the objects on which the social perspective focuses with suspicion, if not hostility.

Nonetheless, nothing I have said so far shows that the tension between liberal political philosophy and the social perspective entails that the two are incompatible. Many political theories have found a home within the broad scope of the liberal tradition, and these theories differ significantly in what they have to say about the relationship between individuals and social systems. It is unlikely that the question whether liberal political philosophy can adopt the social perspective about racial injustice can be answered in a general way, once for all liberal political theories. Instead, the question must be posed with respect to one particular theory, or a set of theories that share a number of significant traits in common.

In the next several chapters, I shall focus not on the classical liberalism of John Locke, John Stuart Mill, or other figures of the historical canon, but on the form of liberalism that has achieved dominance in political philosophy since the early 1970s, namely, welfare liberalism. In particular, I shall focus on the work of the leading advocate of this form of liberalism, namely, John Rawls, and on the work of the most able and insightful reformer of this form of liberalism, namely, Will Kymlicka. I shall examine in detail whether the basic commitments of welfare liberalism permit it to adopt the social perspective on racial injustice. If my conclusions in chapters one and two are correct, then the question whether welfare liberalism can adopt the social perspective will determine whether welfare liberalism can address racial injustice adequately.

Notes

1. U.S. Bureau of the Census, *Fourteenth Census of the United States: State Compendium – Nebraska* (Washington, D.C.: U.S. Government Printing Office, 1925), 37.

2. Pew Partnership for Civic Change, *Celebrating the Past – Charting the Future: Omaha's African American Community* (Omaha, Nebr.: Urban League of Nebraska, 2008), 8; Bruce H. Webster, Jr., and Alemayehu Bishaw, *Income, Earnings, and Poverty Data from the 2006 American Community Survey* (Washington, D.C.: U.S. Government Printing Office, 2007), 20.

3. Elliot Njus, "'Lest We Forget' Our History," *Omaha World-Herald*, Jul. 15, 2009.

4. See, for instance, Nancy Abelmann, *Blue Dreams: Korean Americans and the Los Angeles Riots* (Cambridge, Mass.: Harvard University Press, 1995); Mark Baldassare, ed., *The Los Angeles Riots: Lessons for the Urban Future* (Boulder: Westview, 1994); Robert Gooding-Williams, ed., *Reading Rodney King/Reading Urban Uprising* (New York: Routledge, 1993); Anna Deavere Smith, *Twilight – Los Angeles, 1992 on the Road: A Search for American Character* (New York: Anchor, 1994); and Raphael J. Sonenshein, *Politics in Black and White: Race and Power in Los Angeles* (Princeton: Princeton University Press, 1993).

5. Patrick Strawbridge and Tanya Eiserer, "Police Use of Deadly Force About Average: Fatal Police Shootings," *Omaha World-Herald*, Jul. 23, 2000, Sunrise Edition.

6. Hollis Limprecht, "Centennial Series: Summer of 1966 Was 'Long, Hot' as the Riots Reached Omaha," *Omaha World-Herald*, Jun. 16, 1985, Sunrise Edition.

7. Deborah Alexander, "'The Night Hangs in My Memory, Not Happily.' A George Wallace Presidential Campaign Rally 30 Years Ago Sparked Four Days of Civil Unrest, Left One Person Dead and Polarized Omaha's Race Relations," *Omaha World-Herald*, March 5, 1998, Metro Edition.

8. Hollis Limprecht, "Centennial Series: Summer of 1966 Was 'Long, Hot' as the Riots Reached Omaha," *Omaha World-Herald*, Jun. 16, 1985, Sunrise Edition.

9. Deborah Alexander, "Officers Tell of Ammons Shooting: Sears' and Kister's Versions of Events Differ in the Men's First Public Testimony in the Death," *Omaha World-Herald*, Apr. 12, 2000, Sunrise Edition.

10. Angie Brunkow and C. David Kotok, "Police Reports: Ammons had Loaded Gun in Hand," *Omaha World-Herald*, Jan. 1, 1998, Sunrise Edition. Angie Brunkow, "Officer Sears Indicted: Grand Jury Charges Manslaughter in Ammons Death," *Omaha World-Herald*, Jan. 27, 1998, Sunrise Edition.

11. Cindy Gonzalez, "Councilman Asks: Where Was Camera? Fatal Shooting Among Incidents Not Captured on Video, Brown Says," *Omaha World-Herald*, Oct. 30, 1997, Sunrise Edition.

12. Cindy Gonzalez, "Police Still Putting Together Events that Led to Shooting," *Omaha World-Herald*, Oct. 27, 1997, Metro Edition; Loren Keller and Cindy Gonzalez, "Brown: Keep Cameras Rolling," *Omaha World-Herald*, Nov. 1, 1997, Sunrise Edition; Cindy Gonzalez, "Police Union Defends Decision to Shoot," *Omaha World-Herald*, Nov. 4, 1997, Sunrise Edition.

13. Angie Brunkow, "Judge Seizes Reports in Ammons Shooting," *Omaha World-Herald*, Dec. 30, 1997, Sunrise Edition.

14. Angie Brunkow, "Officer Sears Indicted: Grand Jury Charges Manslaughter in Ammons Death," *Omaha World-Herald*, Jan. 27, 1998, Sunrise Edition.

15. Angie Brunkow, "Sears Lawyer Gets to Review Grand Jury Evidence," *Omaha World-Herald*, Jul. 2, 1998, Sunrise Edition.

16. Angie Brunkow, "Sears Indictment Dismissed: Juror Misconduct Found," *Omaha World-Herald*, Nov. 6, 1998, Sunrise Edition. The makeup of the first grand jury in the Sears case was 16 percent African-American. This is roughly proportionate to the African-American portion of the population of Douglas County, which was 12 percent according to the 2000 US Census.

17. Chris Burbach, "Alternate Juror Not One to Look the Other Way: The Ammons Case is not the First Time Pat Metoyer has Spoken Out When She Has Perceived Injustice," *Omaha World-Herald*, Nov. 8, 1998, Sunrise Edition.

18. Angie Brunkow and C. David Kotok, "Ammons Jury Clears Officers," *Omaha World-Herald*, Jan. 21, 1999, Sunrise Edition.

19. Deborah Alexander, "Civil Trial Pursued in Death: A Lawsuit by the Mother of Marvin Ammons, whom Police Shot in 1997, Goes to Trial Today," *Omaha World-Herald*, Apr. 8, 2000, Bulldog Edition.

20. Deborah Alexander and Toni Heinzl, "Jury Clears 2 Officers in Shooting," *Omaha World-Herald*, Apr. 14, 2000, Sunrise Edition.

21. Karyn Spencer, "Probe Under Way in Slaying by Police," *Omaha World-Herald*, Jul. 20, 2000, Sunrise Edition.

22. Karyn Spencer and Tanya Eiserer, "Prosecutor Eyes Charges. Jansen: No Hasty Decision about Police Shooting," *Omaha World-Herald*, Jul. 21, 2000, Metro Edition.

23. Tanya Eiserer and Karyn Spencer, "Officer Will Be Charged Today in Fatal Shooting," *Omaha World-Herald*, Jul. 26, 2000, Sunrise Edition.

24. Angie Brunkow, "Kruse Charge Thrown Out: After a Manslaughter Count is Dismissed, the Case Continues with Selection of a Grand Jury in the Police Shooting," *Omaha World-Herald*, Aug. 19, 2000, Sunrise Edition.

25. Angie Brunkow and Karyn Spencer, "No Indictment for Kruse: Despite Grand Jury Decision, Officer in Fatal Shooting May Still Face Charges," *Omaha World-Herald*, Sept. 2, 2000, Sunrise Edition.

26. Angie Brunkow, "Grand Jury Records Requested: County Attorney Seeks to Bolster Kruse Case," *Omaha World-Herald*, Sept. 15, 2000, Sunrise Edition.

27. Angie Brunkow, "Access to Kruse Transcripts Denied: A Judge Turns Down a Prosecutor's Request for Grand Jury Documents in the Police Shooting of George Bibbins," *Omaha World-Herald*, Oct. 24, 2000, Sunrise Edition; Robynn Tysver, "Kruse Can Be Charged, Court Says: But Grand Jury Transcripts in the Officer's Killing of George Bibbins Can't Be Reviewed by the Douglas County Attorney," *Omaha World-Herald*, May 31, 2002.

28. Robynn Tysver and Tom Shaw, "Jansen: Kruse Won't Be Charged. The Decision Disappoints the Mother of George Bibins, the Man Killed by the Now-Retired Police Officer," *Omaha World-Herald*, Jun. 1, 2002, Sunrise Edition.

29. Karyn Spencer, "Pension Approved for Kruse," *Omaha World-Herald*, Aug. 17, 2001, Sunrise Edition.

30. Karyn Spencer, "Bibins Slaying Probe Inconclusive: A Police Investigation Finds Officer Jerad Kruse Thought the Chase Victim Had a Gun, But it Fails to Determine Whether the Shooting was Justified," *Omaha World-Herald*, Aug. 29, 2002, Metro Edition.

31. Deborah Alexander and Toni Heinzl, "Jury Clears 2 Officers in Shooting. Lawyer: Verdict Means Claims Against City Will Be Dismissed," *Omaha World-Herald*, Apr. 14, 2000, Sunrise Edition.

32. Cindy Gonzalez, "Police Union Defends Decision to Shoot," *Omaha World-Herald*, Nov. 4, 1997, Sunrise Edition; Karyn Spencer, Tanya Eiserer, and Henry J. Cordes, "Dad: Kruse 'Did What He Had To': Police Officer Charged in Shooting After Chase," *Omaha World-Herald*, Jul. 26, 2000, Metro Edition.

33. Angie Brunkow and C. David Kotok, "Ammons Jury Clears Officers," *Omaha World-Herald*, Jan. 21, 1999, Sunrise Edition.

34. Kimberlé Crenshaw and Gary Peller offer a similar analysis of the verdict in the criminal trial of the Los Angeles police officers who beat Rodney King in "Reel Time/Real Justice," in *Reading Rodney King: Reading Urban Uprising*, ed. R. Gooding-Williams (New York: Routledge, 1993), 56–70.

35. Charles W. Mills, *The Racial Contract* (Ithaca: Cornell University Press, 1997), 36–37.

36. Mills, *The Racial Contract*, 73–77.

37. Mills distinguishes *de jure* from *de facto* white supremacy in *The Racial Contract*, 73.

38. Cindy Gonzalez and Chris Burbach, "Black Leaders Voice Frustration," *Omaha World-Herald*, Jan. 21, 1999, Sunrise Edition.

Chapter Three
The Political Significance
of Social Identity

Philosophers of race and feminist philosophers have long had a complex, tense relationship with liberal political philosophy. On the one hand, many philosophers of race and feminist philosophers are attracted by the liberal ideals of freedom, equality, and fairness because of the critical leverage that these ideals can provide against white supremacy and patriarchy. This is one reason why many advocates of feminism, from the eighteenth century right up to the present, have framed their arguments for women's equality within the liberal tradition.[1] It is also one reason why many contemporary African-American political philosophers are reluctant to leave the liberal tradition entirely, despite their misgivings about many aspects of the tradition.[2]

On the other hand, many philosophers of race and feminist philosophers are repelled by the silence of prominent liberal political philosophers about serious forms of social injustice related to race and gender. For instance, feminist political philosophers began to publish criticisms of John Rawls's 1971 work, *A Theory of Justice*, as early as the mid-1980s.[3] Yet when Rawls published his next major work, *Political Liberalism*, in 1993, he ignored the feminist critical literature on his work almost completely.[4] When Rawls finally did respond to some of the most moderate and sympathetic of the feminist criticisms, those voiced by Susan Moller Okin in *Justice, Gender, and the Family*, his response took the form of a brief section of an article devoted to another topic, and was widely judged as inadequate, even by thinkers otherwise sympathetic to Rawls.[5]

Another source of concern is the deafening silence of the canonical historical and contemporary figures in the liberal tradition of political philosophy on the subject of racial slavery. From the seventeenth century through the nineteenth century, Great Britain and the United States were the leading sites for the theory and practice of liberalism and key players in the trans-Atlantic trade in African slaves. Centuries of participation in the system of racial slavery by two nations that were viewed, by themselves and others, as beacons of liberty in an autocratic world obviously poses pressing questions for British and American liberals alike. Yet, from Locke and Mill to Rawls and Nozick, no major liberal political philosopher has taken up the challenge of answering the questions posed by the legacy of racial slavery. Philosophers of race may justly ask whether a political philosophical tradition that has had so little to say about one of the most gravely unjust social systems that ever existed can be expected to hold the key to undermining white supremacy.[6]

Readers who are critical of the indifference of prominent liberal political philosophers to forms of social injustice related to race and gender might wonder whether this silence simply results from a failure of the liberal thinkers in question to investigate the implications their political ideals have for racial and gender inequality, or whether it results instead from a deeper theoretical flaw that lies within the liberal conceptual framework. Many thinkers who attribute the silence of prominent liberals about racial and gender inequality to deeply rooted features of liberalism's conceptual framework have traced this problem to an assumption about the nature of persons that is sometimes referred to as abstract individualism. Abstract individualism is the assumption that human individuals are atom-like units of which social groups are composed. As such, these individuals are ontologically prior to the societies in which they live. As Alison Jaggar puts it, liberals assume that

> [l]ogically, if not empirically, human individuals could exist outside a social context; their essential characteristics, their needs and interests, their capacities and desires, are given independently of their social context and are not created or even fundamentally altered by that context.[7]

Jaggar argues that this assumption of abstract individualism prevents liberals from addressing the needs and interests of persons which arise from the social contexts in which they live.[8] Similarly, even when Charles W. Mills expresses optimism about the emancipatory potential of liberalism and the social contract tradition, he argues that liberalism must first shed its "misleading social ontology" of "atomistic individualism" in order to realize its potential.[9]

Jaggar also argues that liberalism conceives of human nature not only atomistically, but also egoistically, and that John Rawls's well-known theory of justice is an example of this approach.[10] The parties in Rawls's original position, the contracting situation in which the principles of justice are selected, are defined as abstract individuals who know nothing specific about the society about which they are deliberating and take no interest in one another's interests. Jaggar sees Rawls's definition of the parties in the original position as justified by his assumptions that actual persons' interests are pre-socially defined and primarily egoistic.[11] As a result of these assumptions, Jaggar believes that Rawls's theory of justice focuses narrowly on the individualistic goods of individual rights and liberties, fair shares of social resources, and self-respect, and that this theory is incapable of taking socially conditioned and constructed goods into account. Jaggar then argues that this limitation prevents his theory from addressing serious forms of injustice related to gender, race, and class.[12]

In the preface to *Political Liberalism*, Rawls claims that criticisms such as Jaggar's are based on a misconception regarding his description of the original position. Rawls accuses these critics of confusing his abstract description of the parties in the original position with his conception of actual persons, and of falsely attributing a position of abstract individualism to him as a result.[13] In *Political Liberalism*, Rawls tries to clear up this confusion in two ways. First, he shows that the original position is merely a device of representation and not a free-standing argument for his theory of justice.[14] Second, he demonstrates that his theory actually rests on a conception of the person which differs significantly from the description of the parties in the original position. This conception of the person, which I shall call Rawls's theory of agency, includes his conceptions of the distinctive powers of human agents, the goods that such agents pursue, and the means that they require in order to pursue those goods.[15] Rawls believes that these two clarifications suffice to defend his theory of justice against the above criticisms.

Rawls is probably correct that many of those who have attributed the position of abstract individualism to him have done so in part because they misinterpret his discussion of the original position in *Theory of Justice*.[16] Nevertheless, I shall argue in this chapter that Rawls's reply to his critics — through his articulation of this theory of agency in *Political Liberalism* — makes it more apparent than ever why his theory cannot address various forms of injustice related to cultural identity, race, gender, and other aspects of social identity. I begin by sketching out the theory of agency that Rawls develops in *Political Liberalism* in section one. In section two, I argue that this theory of agency is inadequate to ground a theory of justice that is capable of addressing certain forms of injustice related to cultural identity and race. Specifically, I argue that both threats to the existence of some minority cultures and white supremacy are forms of injustice that Rawls cannot adequately address. In section three, I address one possible reply to my argument based on Rawls's account of the social bases of self-esteem and self-respect. I conclude by discussing briefly the prospects for developing an alternative theory of justice based on a revised version of Rawls's conception of the person.

1. Rawls's Theory of Agency

The overall goal of *Political Liberalism* is to articulate a conception of justice that all reasonable citizens of a well-ordered liberal democratic society can accept, no matter to what overall moral, religious, or philosophical views they subscribe. For this reason, Rawls's political conception of justice cannot be grounded in any particular overall view or comprehensive doctrine that some reasonable citizens could not accept. Rather, it must be based on fundamental ideas implicit within the political culture of a liberal democratic society, which all reasonable members of that society can accept.[17]

Rawls contends that these fundamental ideas are captured by what I am calling his theory of agency, which includes three components: a thin theory of the good, a political conception of the person, and an account of primary goods as citizens' needs.[18] Rawls implicitly makes three important assumptions in developing this theory of agency. These assumptions are (1) that the citizens of a well-ordered society would generally require the same means for moral development and human fulfillment; (2) that those means may be uniformly treated as objects which individuals can possess; and (3) that persons' memberships in groups defined by cultural identity, race, gender, and other aspects of their social identities are politically irrelevant. After I briefly sketch out the three components of Rawls's theory of agency, I shall try to show how this theory entails each of these three assumptions.

The first component of Rawls's theory of agency is his conception of goodness as rationality, which was called the thin theory of the good in *A Theory of Justice*.[19]   This theory is thin because it tries to give an abstract account of the ends that citizens of modern liberal democracies pursue without promoting any particular plan of life or conception of the good over others and without appealing to any particular comprehensive moral, religious, or philosophical doctrine for its justification. In this way, the thin theory of the good aims to capture the basic elements of the various conceptions of the good held by every citizen of a modern liberal democracy, so long as those conceptions meet minimal standards of rationality.

The thin theory of the good involves two claims: (1) that human life and the fulfillment of human needs and purposes are, in general, good; and (2) that rationality is a proper principle of social organization.[20] The first claim is quite weak, as it requires only that the citizens of a modern liberal democracy view their lives and the fulfillment of their needs and purposes as goods worth promoting. The second claim likewise does not imply any strong ideal of efficiency or bureaucratic control, but only the idea that social cooperation should be regulated by certain basic, minimal principles of rationality (e.g., choose the most effective means to a desired end, other things being equal).[21] Taken together, these two claims imply that the goal of social cooperation should be to provide the means required for the preservation of human life and the fulfillment of human needs and purposes through rationally chosen means.

The thin theory of the good plays a dual role in Rawls's political theory. In the first place, it provides the framework for Rawls's account of the primary goods, the all-purpose means to the preservation of life and the fulfillment of needs and purposes that every citizen desires, no matter what else she desires. On his account, these primary goods include rights and liberties, opportunities, and income and wealth.[22] Without such an account, the parties in the original position would have no way of estimating the good of the citizens whom they represent, and so would have no basis from which to choose any particular conception of justice. In the second place, the thin theory of the good helps define the freedom and motivation of the parties in the original position. The parties need such an abstract account of citizens' good to supply their motivation in deliberation without violating the veil of ignorance by giving them particular knowledge of their own determinate conceptions of the good.[23]

The second component of Rawls's theory of agency is his political conception of the person. Rawls intends this conception of the person to be political rather than metaphysical in the sense that it involves only the attributes that a person must have in order to be capable of social cooperation.[24] Rawls takes pains to argue that this political conception of the person does not involve any full-blown metaphysical theory about human nature, the relation of mind and body, ethical or theological virtue, or whatever.[25] As such, this conception of the person is designed to be acceptable to any reasonable citizen of a modern liberal democracy, no matter to what moral, religious, or philosophical doctrine she subscribes. It involves the fundamental idea of the person, which Rawls derives from the conception of social cooperation; the higher-order interests of the person, which Rawls derives from this fundamental idea of the person; and the respects in which citizens consider themselves as free, which Rawls derives from these higher-order interests.[26]

In order to be capable of participating in a system of social cooperation, a person must possess two moral powers: (1) the capacity to form, revise, and pursue a conception of the good over the course of a whole life; and (2) the capacity to have a sense of justice, that is, to have a normally effective desire to act from principles of justice that one would choose under fair conditions of deliberation. In addition, a person must also possess some determinate conception of the good or other, although the nature of this conception may change over the course of a whole life.[27] Unless these requirements can be met, a person's rational advantage cannot be specified and a person cannot reasonably be expected to propose or accept fair terms of social cooperation. In such circumstances, social cooperation, as opposed to socially coordinated activity, cannot take place.

Assuming now that these requirements are met and social cooperation among persons is possible, Rawls derives from them a general account of the higher-order interests of persons, that is, the interests which persons have no matter what other interests they have. Given that the circumstances of justice obtain, social cooperation is both possible and necessary for the fulfillment of persons' conceptions of the good.[28] Thus every person may be assumed to have an interest in participating in social cooperation and in enjoying its fruits, no matter what other interests he has.[29] And since each person must possess the two moral powers and a determinate conception of the good in order for social cooperation to take place, every person may be assumed to have a higher-order interest in possessing the moral powers and a determinate conception of the good. Rawls therefore assigns to each person three higher-order interests: (1) an interest in the full development and free exercise of her capacity to have a conception of the good; (2) an interest in the full development and free exercise of her capacity to have a sense of justice; and (3) an interest in the fulfillment of her conception of the good.[30]

Because citizens of Rawls's well-ordered liberal democratic society recognize that they each have these two moral powers, a determinate but evolving conception of the good, and these three higher-order interests, they consider themselves to be free in three respects. First, they consider themselves free to form, revise, and pursue a conception of the good of their own choosing, without risking the loss of their rights and liberties as citizens by doing so.[31] Second, they consider themselves free to make claims on social institutions on their own merits for the purposes of achieving ends or fulfilling obligations implied by their conceptions of the good. That is, they consider themselves entitled to stake claims to goods that they want (within the bounds of justice) without appealing for justification to institutions' obligations toward society at large, to their positions in a social hierarchy, or to anything else besides their status as moral persons.[32] And third, they consider themselves free to adjust their conceptions of the good in light of what they can reasonably expect to achieve given both the constraints of possibility imposed by the limited available stock of social resources and the demands of the political conception of justice.[33]

The third component of Rawls's theory of agency is his account of the primary goods required for moral development and human fulfillment. This account seeks to identify the means which are generally required for the attainment of the human good.[34] In order to identify them, it depends both upon the thin theory of the good to supply a general and abstract conception of the human good and upon the political conception of the person to supply an account of the higher-order interests of moral persons. The account of the primary goods also depends on two assumptions. First, it assumes that all the citizens of Rawls's well-ordered liberal democratic society affirm the same political conception of the person, so that they share a conception of human beings' higher-order interests. Second, it assumes that those citizens require the same primary goods for the advancement of their conceptions of the good and their higher-order interests.[35] If both of these conditions are met, then sufficient common ground exists for the establishment of a political conception of justice to govern society's cooperative activities. Rawls concludes his account of the primary goods by listing the kinds of primary goods suited to satisfy the higher-order interests of the citizens of a modern liberal democracy: civil and political liberties, powers and prerogatives of offices in social institutions, income and wealth, and the social bases of self-esteem and self-respect.[36]

Once all three components of Rawls's theory of agency are in place, he can use this theory to define the original position, the contracting situation in which abstractly defined parties choose the principles of justice. The ends that the parties pursue in their deliberations are given by the account of citizens' higher-order interests contained in Rawls's political conception of the person. The definition of reasons admissible into the parties' deliberations is given by the account of morally relevant considerations contained in Rawls's discussion of the freedoms of moral persons. And the parties' method of pursuing citizens' higher-order interests is supplied by the account of the primary goods. Since Rawls's theory of agency justifies his definition of the original position, and the definition of the original position determines which principles of justice the parties will choose, Rawls's theory of agency therefore serves as the main argument for his theory of justice. His description of the original position merely illustrates how this argument works, and adds nothing substantive to it.

Now that we have seen how Rawls's theory of agency provides the foundation on which the original position is constructed, it is possible to examine some of the basic assumptions on which the theory depends. First, Rawls explicitly assumes in his account of the primary goods that the citizens of a well-ordered society would generally require the same means for moral development and human fulfillment. Rawls conceives of the well-ordered liberal democratic society as being pluralistic in respect of citizens' differing conceptions of the good and the various comprehensive doctrines which they use to interpret those conceptions. But Rawls also conceives of this society as homogeneous in respect of the kinds of means these citizens would require to pursue their conceptions of the good and to secure their higher-order interests.[37] The importance of these assumptions about homogeneity will become clear later, in section two of this chapter.

Second, Rawls's account of the primary goods arbitrarily limits the scope of the means to moral development and human fulfillment by treating them exclusively as objects of individuals' possession. Some of these goods, including income and wealth, are paradigmatic examples of material possessions which individuals can own and control. But all of them, including the relevant rights, liberties, powers, and prerogatives, can be distributed among individuals who can possess and exercise them at their pleasure. Rawls's account of the primary goods assumes that social justice amounts to the equitable distribution of such *things* across society. If the primary goods could not be conceived of as things, at least in some abstract sense, it would not be possible to make sense of the idea that we can check to see how equitably they are distributed across society.

Third, despite Rawls's protests that his views are neutral between metaphysical theories of the person, he does assume an individualistic social ontology. As mentioned above, Rawls's account of the primary goods contains only goods which individuals can possess, exercise, or enjoy, including individual rights and liberties, income, and wealth. Additionally, Rawls assumes that individual persons' identifications with various groups within society are either voluntarily formed or politically irrelevant. In the section of *Political Liberalism* entitled "The Political Conception of the Person," Rawls divides persons' identities into two parts, a public or institutional identity and a moral or non-institutional identity.[38] A person's public identity depends only on her having the two moral powers and a determinate conception of the good, while her moral identity depends on the voluntary associations, affections, and loyalties which she freely forms and dissolves as she pleases.[39] Rawls claims that only public identity is politically relevant, because what a person needs in order to secure her higher-order interests depends solely on her status as a full, equal moral agent. A person's memberships in social groups defined by, for instance, culture, race, and gender are not part of her public identity, on Rawls's account, since they are not part of her status as a moral agent. Nor are they part of her moral identity, since they are not freely chosen and withdrawn.[40] Rawls therefore treats social groups such as those defined by culture, race, and gender as morally arbitrary collections, and assigns no political significance to individuals' memberships in such groups.[41] Rawls's social ontology may thus be characterized as individualistic both in respect of his conception of social goods as individuals' possessions and in respect of his view that persons' memberships in groups defined along lines of social identity are morally arbitrary and politically insignificant.

2. Injustices Related to Cultural Membership and Race

Contrary to Rawls's assumptions about agents, I maintain that individuals' memberships in different social groups do affect their chances to develop their moral powers and to fulfill their conceptions of the good. In order to show how this claim contradicts Rawls's theory of agency, I must develop the concept of a social group. In what follows, I will use the terms "social group" and "social identity" as terms of art with meanings that are narrower than the ones assigned to them in everyday language.

The concept of a social group may be defined by contradistinction from the concept of an aggregate and the concept of an association.[42] An aggregate is an arbitrary collection of persons who normally are not consciously identified as members of that collection by themselves or others. Thus an aggregate may be defined on the basis of any arbitrarily chosen characteristic shared by a number of persons, such as having an odd-numbered street address, having been born in a certain month, or giving a certain answer to a survey question. People would not normally identify themselves or others as members of a group defined in such an arbitrary way except in a society that assigned special importance to one of these characteristics. Indeed, a person may be a member of an aggregate whether or not anyone realizes that she is. For this reason, membership in aggregates does not play a significant role in defining a person's social identity, that is, the way a person is normally consciously identified by herself and others.

An association, by contrast, is a group formed by individuals who have joined it voluntarily. Modern liberal democracies abound with associations formed for political, social, occupational, and religious purposes, such as the National Association for the Advancement of Colored People, the Benevolent and Protective Order of Elks, the Teamsters Union, and the Roman Catholic Church. While voluntary membership is the defining characteristic of associations, some associations are more voluntary than others. For instance, since parents tend to pass on their religious beliefs to their children as part of their upbringing, persons tend to adopt the religion of their parents if they accept any religion at all. As a result, a person may never intentionally choose to become a member of their parents' church, synagogue, temple, or mosque, but may rather be socialized into membership and remain a member more out of habit than as a result of choice. Nevertheless, membership in associations is fundamentally voluntary because entrance into and exit from an association is a matter of choice.

In the technical sense in which I use the term "social group," a social group is unlike an association insofar as one does not choose to become a member of such a group, but rather discovers oneself already to be a member. This is the case, for instance, with groups defined along lines of racial and gender identity. A social group also differs from an aggregate insofar as a person's membership in a social group plays an important role in determining how others see her. Thus groups defined along lines of race count as social groups in the US and other societies where racial identification is socially significant, although they might count instead as aggregates in another, hypothetical society not rent by racial divisions. The crucial features of social groups for my purposes are (1) the social significance of membership in these groups and (2) the difficulty or impossibility of choosing to become or cease to be a member of such a group and thus to avoid incurring the stigma or the privilege of group membership. Social groups are distinguished from aggregates in virtue of (1) and from associations in virtue of (2).

In the context of the United States, the best examples of social groups are probably racial groups. A person has no choice about what race he belongs to, and the ingrained, persistent white supremacy of American society ensures that his race will play an extremely important role in his social identity. Membership in gender groups plays an equally important role in people's social identities and is not initially a matter of choice, but people can transgress the boundaries of gender through the practice of homosexuality, transvestitism, or transsexuality. Membership in groups defined by sexual orientation may also involve a degree of choice, since although a person cannot choose what sexual impulses to feel, she can exercise a limited degree of choice about which sexual impulses to focus or act upon. But since this ability affords persons control only over their sexual behavior and not over their sexual orientation, groups such as heterosexuals, gays, and lesbians are better understood as social groups than as associations. This point can be emphasized by considering the difference between being a lesbian, a gay man, or a bisexual woman or man, on the one hand, and belonging to the Gay, Lesbian, and Straight Education Network, on the other.

Groups defined by economic and social class cross the boundary between social groups and aggregates. In a society where social and economic mobility is possible, class membership is somewhat less permanent and slightly more voluntary than membership in race and gender groups. But it is important to distinguish between economic class conceived as an aspect of social identity and a determinant of how people see themselves and one another, on the one hand, and a Marxist conception of economic class, which is defined by a person's relationship to the ownership of the means of production, on the other. In the first sense, the working class is a social group whose members are consciously identified as a group by themselves and others. In the second, Marxist sense, the working class is more like an aggregate than a social group because its existence is completely independent of whether or not anyone identifies its members as standing in the relevant relation to the means of production, since it is defined in terms of economic relations rather than social identity. This does not mean that economic classes defined along Marxist lines lack political significance, but only that they possess political significance, assuming they do, for different reasons than social groups do.

It should be clear that while the concept of a social group can be distinguished from the concepts of an aggregate and an association, these concepts blend into one another around their edges. As a result, the claim that any particular collection of persons is a social group will be contestable, since being a social group is a matter of more/less, not either/or. Nevertheless, it does seem clear that on this conception, groups defined along lines of race, gender, sexuality, and class are in fact social groups in American society. Membership in such groups is currently more involuntary than voluntary, and plays a significant role in the way people identify themselves and are identified by others. Thus in this context, I will treat African-Americans, white Americans, Asian-Americans, Latinas and Latinos, Native Americans, men, women, heterosexual men, heterosexual women, gays, lesbians, bisexuals, middle-class persons, and working class persons as social groups.

While race, gender, class, and sexual identity can be kept conceptually distinct in theoretical discussions, they cannot be kept practically distinct in people's lives. People's experiences cannot, for instance, be separated into those determined by their racial identity and those determined by the gender identity, since a person may be, say, an African-American woman, but cannot be simply an African-American or simply a woman. For this reason, it is important to keep in mind throughout this chapter that although I may speak of African-Americans as a social group, I do not mean to claim that the members of this group share a common racial essence as the basis of their group identity. Particular African-Americans experience their racial identities differently, partly as a result of their different gender, class, and sexual identities. Social groups overlap with one another, and different aspects of a person's social identity cannot be experientially separated like the beads of a pop-bead necklace. They can, nevertheless, be separated conceptually for the purposes of analysis.[43]

For our purposes, then, a social group may be defined as any collection of persons such that (1) these persons are consciously identified as members of that group by themselves and others, (2) they do not initially choose to be members of that group, but rather discover themselves already to be such, and (3) they either are not capable of exiting the group or are capable of doing so only with great difficulty. On this basis, a person's social identity may be defined as the tapestry of social groups to which she belongs. Rawls's theory of agency clearly assumes that a person's social identity is politically irrelevant, since he maintains that the only facet of personal identity which affects considerations of justice in any way is public or institutional identity, that is, her identity as an agent possessing the two moral powers and a determinate conception of the good.[44] Rawls's failure to address the political significance of social identity prevents him from developing an adequate account of the means required for moral development and human fulfillment, in several respects. This can be shown through an examination of Rawls's three assumptions, discussed at the end of section one of this chapter.

The first assumption is that all citizens require the same kinds of primary goods in order to secure their higher-order interests and pursue their conceptions of the good. I contend, to the contrary, that members of different social groups may require different means for the development of their moral powers and the development and pursuit of their conceptions of the good. Rawls has already conceded a specific instance of this general objection in his updated account of the primary goods in *Political Liberalism*. There, Rawls allows that persons whose physical capacities are reduced beyond a basic minimum level of functioning by either illness or accident may need a greater index of primary goods than those with normal physical capacities.[45]

But while some social groups may merely need more of the same primary goods that everyone else has, others may need different kinds of primary goods. Consider the members of a threatened minority culture, such as aboriginal persons in any of a number of countries or the Québécois in Canada. Many members of such cultures depend on the continued existence of their culture as the context of choice in which they develop their moral powers and develop and pursue their conceptions of the good.[46] Because a person's culture is the context in which she develops and exercises her ability to have a conception of the good and a sense of justice, the continued existence of a person's culture is a necessary condition of that person's development and exercise of these moral powers. To conceive of a culture as something like a lifestyle that the members of a certain ethnic or linguistic group choose to share is terribly inadequate. A person's culture is the context in which he makes moral, religious, social, and lifestyle choices, and in which he has reasons for choosing some forms of life over others. Without the existence of culture as a context for choice, there would be no rational grounds for choice. Thus when a minority culture disappears, whether through assimilation, genocide, or whatever, many former members of that culture may no longer be able to make sense of their lives. Some may assimilate successfully and even happily into a majority culture, but this is always difficult for others. The disappearance of their culture is an obstacle to the fulfillment of what Rawls calls the higher-order interests of the latter group.

If all the members of a threatened minority culture are to satisfy their higher-order interests, then they must have the chance to live out their lives as members of this culture, which significantly shapes their social identities. If their culture is to continue to exist and to avoid assimilation into the dominant culture of the majority which surrounds them, then this culture will require special protections against assimilation. Members of the dominant culture do not need the same special protections for their own culture because the existence of their culture, and thus their higher-order interests, is not threatened in the way that the existence of the minority culture is.[47]

Note that these special protections for minority cultures are not justified by appeal to the specific conceptions of the good that members of minority cultures happen to have. Rather, they are justified by appeal to these people's higher-order interests in being able to form a conception of the good and a sense of justice at all. These are interests that we all have simply in virtue of being moral persons, and not in virtue of having one particular conception of the good or another. Nor is it the case that the justification of special protection for threatened minority cultures requires that every existing culture be preserved in its current form at all costs. Certainly every culture's life must be conducted within the limits of justice, and those cultures that cannot persist without grossly transgressing those limits are not deserving of protection.[48] Nonetheless, if the death of a culture involves the loss of an irreplaceable context which alone enables its members to make life choices, then to cause or allow a culture to die is at least a *prima facie* injustice to its members.

Examples of special protections that might be provided for members of threatened minority cultures include the right to some form of self-government, the provision of lands suitable to their distinctive forms of life, and bilingual education. Most of these special provisions would involve some restrictions on the rights and liberties of non-members of these groups and some redistribution of non-members' income and wealth. Even the simple provision of reserved lands to aboriginal peoples, for instance, requires some restrictions on others' freedom of movement and choice of residence and some public expenditure that must largely be borne by others. No matter what form they take, special protections for threatened minority cultures are bound to involve allotting different primary goods to the members of different social groups. Different allotments for members of different groups need not be unfair or unjust. In this case, treating members of different groups as equals involves treating them differently in some respects.[49]

As I showed in section one of this chapter, Rawls is committed to satisfying equally all citizens' higher-order interests in the development of their moral powers and the pursuit of their conceptions of the good, insofar as every moral person's higher-order interests count equally from the point of view of the parties in the original position. This does not mean that Rawls is committed to ensuring that every citizen's conception of the good is satisfied equally. Indeed, under conditions of scarcity that are characteristic of the circumstances of justice, it may well be that some citizens' conceptions of the good can be satisfied only to a limited degree. This might be the case, for instance, for citizens whose conceptions of the good involved the consumption of luxury goods that are priced beyond the means of all the citizens of a society whose distribution of wealth is regulated by Rawls's Difference Principle.[50] Rawls is, however, committed to providing all citizens with the resources they require in order to have fair equality of opportunity to develop their moral powers and to pursue their conceptions of the good within the limits of justice. If the continued existence of one's culture as the context in which one is able to make life choices is required to make possible this development and this pursuit, then presumably Rawls is committed to place a priority on providing the resources necessary to ensure the culture's continued existence.

Nevertheless, Rawls flatly refuses to sanction the assignment of different rights or liberties to members of different social groups. Rawls acknowledges that this refusal may create political and social conditions that will be inhospitable to some ways of life. He views the death of these ways of life as perhaps regrettable, but certainly not in and of itself unjust.[51] In any case, he believes that to preserve such ways of life by affording special protections to their adherents would be too socially divisive to consider.[52] If members of threatened minority cultures cannot preserve their own cultures by using their equal basic rights and liberties and their fair shares of primary goods, then Rawls is content to see minority cultures die off, however great the cost to members of those cultures may be.

To this I have two replies. The first reply is that it is worth noting that any demand for social justice risks causing social divisions. This is as true of Rawls's call to redistribute income and wealth according to the Difference Principle as it is of the call for protection of threatened minority cultures by members of those cultures.[53] If concern about social divisiveness generally counts as an insuperable objection to proposed social reforms, then we must simply affirm the status quo as being the best we can hope for in the absence of society-wide consensus upon a certain social reform program. To affirm this would be effectively to abandon the pursuit of social justice altogether. If the redistribution of income and wealth according to the Difference Principle is likely to cause less social division than the protection of threatened minority cultures, this is because a broader cross-section of the citizens of the post-industrial democracies stand to benefit from the former than from the latter. But even if this is true, it does not show that the former is more just than the latter, but only that the former is likely to be more popular than the latter.

In order to defend an unpopular proposal such as the protection of threatened minority cultures, it will be necessary to convince citizens that their cultures are not merely optional lifestyle accessories, but irreplaceable contexts that enable their members to make moral and personal life choices at all. To convince citizens who are members of secure dominant cultures of this conclusion will not be easy. This would not, however, be the first time that liberals have undertaken to expand citizens' conception of the necessary conditions for a decent life.

During the twentieth century, the post-industrial democracies have generally moved away from a conception of these conditions that was defined almost exclusively in terms of negative rights to a conception that includes the positive right to at least a decent minimum of income and health care. In order to accomplish this shift in public opinion, liberal advocates of a welfare state had to convince members of the middle and upper economic classes that the economic resources they took for granted were a necessary condition of a decent life to which all were entitled as a matter of justice. This argument took a long time to win, and the victory may yet be eroded by a movement back toward the more negative conception of freedom. Nonetheless, the very fact that the argument was won at all shows that incremental change in a society's conception of the necessary conditions for a decent life can take place without destroying social unity.

The second reply to Rawls is that the death of a culture is, in fact, in and of itself unjust if it is an irreplaceable context that many of its members require as a necessary condition for the development of their moral powers and the pursuit of their conceptions of the good. If the continued existence of one's culture is such a necessary condition for the satisfaction of one's higher-order interests, then to live out one's life within that culture is not a lifestyle choice, but a precondition for being able to make lifestyle choices and other moral decisions. Taking culture seriously as being part of what enables people to work out how they want to live requires us to take the defense of threatened cultures seriously when we construct our account of what social justice requires.

Anthony Appiah objects to this argument in a way similar to Rawls, arguing that cultural membership cannot be a primary social good because no one can be deprived of it. Even residents of refugee camps, he argues do belong to a culture, like it or not. And if no one can be deprived of the good of cultural membership, then it is pointless to argue about whether the good is distributed fairly.[54] Appiah is correct, of course, to say that every life that is human in a sense that is more than merely biological involves some sort of cultural context. He errs, however, in claiming that that people's need for the good of cultural membership is simply a need to belong to some culture or other. What people do in fact need is to belong to a culture in which they can make sense of themselves and their choices. In order to play the role of a framework for choice, a culture must be sufficiently vibrant to provide its members with a context that helps make sense of their lives. A culture that is pushed to the brink of extinction by genocide, political oppression, or economic deprivation is unlikely to be sufficiently vibrant to play this role.

Members of threatened minority cultures require special provisions of primary goods in order to preserve their cultures and to secure their higher-order interests, but Rawls's theory of justice expressly forbids this.   This case illustrates the inability of Rawls's political theory to capture the significance of persons' social identities for determining the just distribution of primary goods. In examining this case, I have followed the lead of Will Kymlicka, a liberal political philosopher whose work on cultural membership and liberal citizenship shares with Rawls the view that social justice is fundamentally a distributive matter. In what follows, I shall examine a case of racial injustice that Kymlicka does not address.

The second basic assumption of Rawls's theory of agency is that the means to the fulfillment of persons' higher-order interests may be treated as things, that is, as objects of individuals' possession, such as income, wealth, rights, and liberties. Even if this reified conception of the means to moral development and human fulfillment were adequate to express the needs of members of dominant social groups, such as white males in American society, it would not be adequate to express the needs of the members of many subordinate social groups.

Imagine, for the sake of argument, that contemporary American society were transformed so as to satisfy Rawls's principles of justice, but remained the same in all other respects.   Now consider the situation of African-Americans within such a well-ordered society.   Since African-Americans would be full and equal citizens of a well-ordered society, they would each enjoy a fully adequate and equal complement of basic civil and political rights and liberties and an index of primary goods that would satisfy the Difference Principle.[55] In Rawls's eyes, their higher-order interests in the development of their moral powers and the pursuit of their conceptions of the good would therefore be secure. Indeed, there can be little doubt that most African-Americans would be far better off in this transformed version of US society than they are in the actual one.

Nevertheless, white Americans, who would still constitute the dominant social group in this society, might still adopt an attitude of benevolent, condescending racism toward African-Americans.[56] That is, white Americans might despise African-Americans, regarding their habits, beliefs, and practices as inferior to their own. While they would acknowledge African-Americans as human persons with moral capacities potentially equal to their own, whites might nevertheless perceive them as constrained or impaired by their backward habits, beliefs, and practices, and might treat them as needing instruction and correction from whites in order to overcome their barbaric or brutish tendencies.[57] As a result, African-Americans would suffer degrading treatment at the hands of whites, although at least their basic civil and political liberties would be secure. It is also likely that they would be viewed as unsuited for social positions requiring intelligence, refinement, trustworthiness, and self-control, and that they would consequently end up being represented dispropor-tionately among the ranks of the economically disadvantaged. The Difference Principle, however, would presumably prevent their economic disadvantage from approaching the desperate poverty in which many African-Americans currently live.

The African-Americans could not, of course, assimilate easily to the habits, beliefs, and practices of the dominant group, which are second nature to whites as a result of their different upbringing and socialization. If they should try to assimilate to the dominant group, they would be subject to constant suspicion and paranoid monitoring, and every slip back into old habits would horribly confirm their "true" nature as barbarians or brutes in the eyes of whites. Even the lucky few who assimilated completely and shook off all of their racially marked habits, beliefs, and practices would be indelibly associated with the black race by the color of their skin. And whites would use their very success in assimilation to reprove other African-Americans, saying, "If he can do it, why can't you?"

What do the African-Americans of this example require in order to secure their higher-order interests and to pursue their conceptions of the good? Nothing less than a complete transformation of white supremacist American culture into a culture that values not only African-American persons but also their habits, beliefs, and practices equally with whites'. Unfortunately for Rawls's theory, guaranteeing individual African-Americans free exercise of their basic rights and larger indices of primary goods will not accomplish this cultural transformation. Transforming the denigrating images and values that American culture associates with African-Americans is not simply a matter of distributing some *thing* more equitably across American society. So long as the racist images and values associated with African-Americans do not lead whites to deny African-Americans their equal basic rights and liberties and their fair shares of primary goods, Rawls requires the liberal state to refrain from aiding African-Americans by interfering with whites' pursuit of their white supremacist conceptions of the good.

Let me offer an example of one political program that might help bring about such a transformation. One political project that might play a role in this cultural transformation is a program of anti-white supremacist public education that would aim to help citizens understand how the cultural construction of people's social identities affects their standing in society and their chances in life. Such an educational program would not treat white supremacy merely as a set of prejudicial attitudes that some people have towards members of other races, but rather as a system of power relationships that creates and maintains the dominance of some racial groups over others. In particular, such a program should treat derogatory cultural images of members of subordinate groups not as "mere ideas" or "only words" which, unlike concrete sticks and stones, can never hurt the members of groups to whom they are applied.[58] Rather, such a program should aim to reveal how such images justify and reinforce the practices and institutions that create and sustain white supremacy in the US.

Such an anti-white supremacist education program can be justified by appeal to African-Americans' need for the full, equal respect that is due to them on account of their status as moral persons if they are to fulfill their higher-order interests and to have a fair chance to pursue their conceptions of the good. If the institutions, practices, and power relationships within a society unfairly impede the members of subordinate racial groups from fulfilling their higher-order interests and pursuing their conceptions of the good, then justice demands that those institutions, practices, and power relationships must be transformed. Since this transformation is demanded by justice, and an anti-white supremacist education program is one important step that could be taken toward bringing such a transformation about, it would be justifiable for the state to support and fund such a program with tax funds. Education alone could not bring this transformation about, but such a state-supported education program would be one step in the right direction.

The example of white supremacy in the United States illustrates that members of different social groups may require not only different amounts and kinds of primary goods in order to secure their higher-order interests, but also other sorts of means that cannot be treated as objects of individuals' possession, as Rawlsian primary goods can. In this way it illustrates again the failure of Rawls's theory of agency to capture the significance of persons' social identities for determining the nature of justice.

The third basic assumption of Rawls's theory of agency is that persons' social identities are unrelated to the means which they require in order to attain human fulfillment and moral development, and are therefore politically irrelevant. The above criticisms of Rawls's first two assumptions also demonstrate the falsehood of this third assumption. The need of members of threatened minority cultures to preserve those cultures in order to secure their higher-order interests is just one case in which persons' social identities help determine the kinds of primary goods they require. And African-Americans' need for the cultural transformation of white supremacist American society demonstrates that members of some social groups require means for moral development and human fulfillment which cannot be characterized as objects of individuals' possession on the model of Rawlsian primary goods. These two types of cases illustrate the crucial significance of social identity for concerns about justice. No theory that fails to take account of this significance can adequately define the nature of justice.

A brief discussion of Tommie Shelby's recent work on the idea of black solidarity will help me clarify what I do and do not mean when I say that social identity is crucially significant for concerns about justice. Shelby makes a compelling argument for the claim that African-Americans need not embrace their racial identity or their cultural identity as African-American in order to win emancipation from racial oppression.[59] In fact, Shelby argues that attempts to require African-Americans to embrace a common racial or cultural identity as an essential part of their personal identities is more likely to lead to infighting about who is really black, or black enough, than it is to lead to African-Americans making common cause to resist racial oppression.[60] By contrast, Shelby argues that it is crucial for African-Americans both to recognize that they are all subject to common forms of racial oppression precisely because they are African-American and to act in solidarity with one another to resist this oppression.[61]

It is in this latter sense, rather than the former sense, that I maintain that social identity is crucial to concerns of social justice. I have argued that people's social identities play a significant role in determining the social conditions under which they can achieve moral development and human fulfillment. People need to recognize the role that their social identities play in determining what these conditions are and to act collectively in order to bring the conditions in question into existence. They do not, however, need to embrace every aspect of their social identity as an essential part of their personal identity in order to bring about justice in this way.

3. Rawls on the Social Bases of Self-Respect

At this point I must address an objection to my critique of Rawls's theory which is based on Rawls's account of the social bases of self-esteem and self-respect. These social bases are among the primary social goods which persons require in order to fulfill their higher-order interests, and Rawls repeatedly acknowledges that they are perhaps the most important of the primary social goods.[62] Readers sympathetic with Rawls may hope that the inclusion of the social bases of self-esteem and self-respect within Rawls's account of the primary goods may allow this account to include, say, a non-white supremacist culture within the index of primary goods to which African-Americans are entitled. After all, living in a non-white supremacist culture is surely one of the social conditions that African-Americans require in order to achieve self-esteem and self-respect. If it were the case that Rawls would consider a non-white supremacist culture to be one of the social bases of self-esteem and self-respect, then Rawls's theory of justice would accept the creation of a non-white supremacist culture as a requirement for the fulfillment of African-Americans' higher-order interests. In that case, my claim that Rawls's theory does not address African-Americans' need for the creation of a non-racist culture would be false.

Rawls's account of the social bases of self-esteem and self-respect is, however, more restrictive than this. Rawls maintains that a person possesses the social bases of self-esteem and self-respect whenever the two principles of justice are satisfied and there is "some association (one or more) to which he belongs and within which the activities that are rational for him are publicly affirmed by others."[63] So Rawls would say that African-Americans would possess the social bases of self-esteem and self-respect if they had full and equal complements of basic rights and liberties, fair shares of the primary social goods, and membership in one or more associations in which they could pursue their interests and find their pursuits affirmed. But African-Americans could possess all these goods and still be unable to secure their higher-order interests and fulfill their conceptions of the good because of the white supremacist culture in which they live. Rawls's account of the social bases of self-esteem and self-respect therefore does not address African-Americans' need for the creation of a non-white supremacist culture.

It would, of course, be possible to deviate from Rawls's expressed views by denying that a person possesses the social bases of self-esteem and self-respect whenever she has the requisite rights and liberties, social resources, and membership in associations in which she can pursue her special interests. One might then supplement Rawls's theory of justice with a broader account of the social bases of self-esteem and self-respect, which could include, for instance, a non-white supremacist culture as one necessary means to self-esteem and self-respect. It is worth noting, however, that such a revised theory could no longer treat the primary social goods as objects which individuals can possess and enjoy. Nor could it claim, as Rawls does, that social justice is simply a matter of the equitable distribution of such objects across society. For this reason, such a revision of Rawls would not constitute a defense of his theory as he has expressed it in *A Theory of Justice* and *Political Liberalism*, but the first step toward the creation of a new theory.

4. Prospects for a Post-Rawlsian Theory of Justice and Agency

The objections to Rawls's theory of agency that I have considered suggest that any adequate theory of justice must account for the political significance of social identity. Such a theory might very well adopt a Rawlsian account of persons' moral powers and higher-order interests, since the objections that I have raised do not touch the nature of these powers or interests, but only the nature of the conditions under which persons are able to develop these powers and secure these interests. An alternative theory of justice based on Rawls's political conception of the person would, however, need to provide an account of the necessary conditions for moral development and human fulfillment that could stand as an alternative to Rawls's account of primary goods. Rawls's account contains several individualistic assumptions about agents that prevent him from showing how white supremacy and threats to the existence of minority cultures pose obstacles to moral development and human fulfillment for members of subordinate races and minority cultures.

It is these individualistic assumptions, and not Rawls's description of the original position, that prevent his theory from identifying white supremacy, patriarchy, and other forms of oppression as unjust. The two parts of Rawls's theory are, however, closely linked, since the original position is defined on the basis of Rawls's political conception of the person even though this conception of the person is not identical with the description of the parties in the original position. Thus, those who criticize Rawls for espousing what Jaggar calls abstract individualism are on target in claiming that individualism is a crucial problem for Rawls's theory of justice, despite his protestations in *Political Liberalism*. They simply miss the mark in attributing to Rawls a form of individualism even more extreme than the one he espouses, and in locating that individualism primarily in the description of the original position rather than in the fundamental assumptions about persons which ground that description.

A reader who is generally sympathetic to liberalism might wonder whether a political theory might remain grounded within the liberal tradition and yet avoid making the individualistic assumptions that prevent Rawls from addressing fully the various forms of social injustice that operate along lines of culture, race, and gender. One reason for optimism about this possibility is the fact that one of the two main criticisms lodged against Rawls in this chapter was developed by a fellow liberal, Canadian political philosopher Will Kymlicka. The fact that Kymlicka criticizes at least some of the limitations of Rawls's theory of justice on grounds that are clearly liberal has caused many progressive liberals to hope that they can develop a liberal theory that will adequately address the various forms of domination and oppression that act along lines of culture, race, gender, and other dimensions of social identity. Another reason for optimism is that Tommie Shelby's argument in support of a form of black solidarity that he calls pragmatic black nationalism, with which I expressed strong sympathy earlier in this chapter, is intended to be consistent with Rawls's political liberalism.[64] I have argued that Rawls's political liberalism is not adequate to address all forms of social injustice, but perhaps Shelby and others would hold out hope that a modified liberal theory of distributive justice might be immune to my arguments.

In the next chapter, however, I shall argue that so long as liberal political theorists continue to conceive of social justice in strictly distributive terms, as Kymlicka and many other contemporary liberals do, they will remain committed to a form of individualism that will prevent them from addressing adequately the full range of social injustice. Other liberal political philosophers do not conceive of social justice in strictly distributive terms. I will discuss the prospects of these non-distributive liberal theories of justice at the end of the next chapter.

Notes

1. Early liberal feminists include Mary Wollstonecraft, *A Vindication of the Rights of Woman* (New York: Penguin Books, 1992); Harriett Taylor Mill, "Enfranchisement of Women," in *Essays on Sex Equality*, ed. A. S. Rossi (Chicago: University of Chicago Press, 1970); and John Stuart Mill, *The Subjection of Women*, ed. S. M. Okin (Indianapolis: Hackett, 1988). For more recent versions of liberal feminism, see Susan Moller Okin, *Justice, Gender, and the Family* (New York: Basic Books, 1989), and Amy R. Baehr, ed., *Varieties of Liberal Feminism* (Lanham, Md.: Rowman & Littlefield, 2004).

2. Kevin M. Graham, "Race and the Limits of Liberalism," *Philosophy of the Social Sciences* 32, no. 2 (Jun. 2002), 237–238.

3. John Rawls, *A Theory of Justice*, rev. ed. (Cambridge, Mass.: Harvard University Press, 1999). For feminist criticisms of *Theory of Justice*, see Karen Green, "Rawls, Women, and the Priority of Liberty," *Australasian Journal of Philosophy*, supp. vol. 64 (1986), 26–36; Susan Moller Okin, "Justice and Gender," *Philosophy & Public Affairs* 16 (1987), 42–72; Sibyl Schwartzenbach, "Rawls and Ownership: The Forgotten Category of Reproductive Labor," in *Science, Morality, and Feminist Theory*, ed. M. P. Hanen & K. Nielsen, *Canadian Journal of Philosophy*, supp. vol. 13 (1987); Okin, *Justice, Gender, and the Family* (New York: Basic Books, 1989); Okin, "Reason and Feeling in Thinking about Justice," *Ethics* 99, no. 2 (Jan. 1989), 229–249. Amy R. Baehr, "Toward a New Feminist Liberalism: Okin, Rawls, and Habermas," *Hypatia* 11, no. 1 (1996), 49–66;

4. Rawls, *Political Liberalism* (New York: Columbia University Press, 1993).

5. Okin has criticized Rawls in a number of places, but the best overview of her critique can be found in *Justice, Gender, and the Family* (New York: Basic Books, 1989). Rawls's reply to Okin can be found in "The Idea of Public Reason Revisited," *University of Chicago Law Review* 64 (1997), 765–807. One critical view of Rawls's reply is articulated in Martha Nussbaum, "The Future of Feminist Liberalism," *Proceedings & Addresses of the American Philosophical Association* 74, no. 2 (2000), 59–67.

6. Lucius T. Outlaw, Jr., *On Race and Philosophy* (New York: Routledge, 1996), 43.

7. Alison Jaggar, *Feminist Politics and Human Nature* (Totowa, N.J.: Rowman & Allanheld, 1983), 29.

8. Jaggar, *Feminist Politics*, 42–44.

9. Mills, *From Class to Race*, 219.

10. Rawls articulates this theory in *Theory of Justice* and in a slightly revised form in *Political Liberalism*.

11. Jaggar, *Feminist Politics*, 31.

12. Others who have discussed this problem in Rawls's work include Kai Nielsen, *Equality and Liberty: A Defense of Radical Egalitarianism* (Totowa, N. J.: Rowman & Allanheld, 1985); Okin, *Justice, Gender, and the Family*; and Iris Marion Young, *Justice and the Politics of Difference* (Princeton: Princeton University Press, 1990).

13. Rawls, *Political Liberalism*, xxix. It should be noted that Rawls is not specifically addressing Jaggar's criticisms of his view in this passage.

14. Rawls, *Political Liberalism*, 23–28.

15. Rawls scholars will note that "theory of agency" is not one of Rawls's own technical terms, but one of my own devising. I trust that this neologism will not cause any undue confusion. I have introduced this term in order to give a name to Rawls's

conception of the subjects to whom his theory of justice applies, which he develops in various different places in *Political Liberalism*.

16. Even granting this point to Rawls, I do not think it is completely misguided to attribute a position similar to abstract individualism to him. As I will make clear in section one, I believe that there are several important ways in which Rawls's conception of human persons is individualistic. Moreover, Rawls understands those individuals' moral and political identities in abstraction from their memberships in groups defined by, for instance, gender, race, and class. If my interpretation of Rawls is correct, then it would not be unfair to describe his conception of the person as abstract individualism. But I would mean by this term something significantly different from what Jaggar means in her discussion of Rawls in *Feminist Politics and Human Nature*. In order to avoid confusion on this point, I deliberately avoid using this term.

17. Rawls, *Political Liberalism*, 13–15.

18. Rawls, *Political Liberalism*, 29–35, 178–190.

19. Rawls, *Theory*, 347–350, 365–372. Rawls also discusses this conception of the good in the second section of the fifth lecture in *Political Liberalism*, 177–178.

20. Rawls, *Political Liberalism*, 177.

21. See Rawls, *Political Liberalism*, 50.

22. Rawls, *Theory*, 79.

23. Rawls, *Political Liberalism*, 178.

24. Rawls, *Political Liberalism*, 18–20.

25. Rawls distinguishes political and metaphysical conceptions of the person in *Political Liberalism*, 29, n. 30.

26. On the distinction between social cooperation and socially coordinated activity, see *Political Liberalism*, 16; on Rawls's conception of citizens' higher-order interests, see *Political Liberalism*, 73–75; and on the respects in which citizens consider themselves as free, see *Political Liberalism*, 29–35. In the section of *Political Liberalism* entitled "The Political Conception of the Person," Rawls only discusses the last of these three features of persons, namely, the respects in which citizens consider themselves as free. But all of these features are aspects of Rawls's idea of moral personhood, and the name "the political conception of the person" is as convenient a title as any to give to the whole package. I hope that this slight deviation from Rawls's usage will not cause any undue confusion.

27. Rawls, *Political Liberalism*, 19.

28. Rawls distinguishes between objective and subjective circumstances of justice and discusses both types of circumstances in *Theory*, 109–112. In *Political Liberalism*, he focuses primarily on the subjective circumstances of justice, and he discusses these circumstances in some detail on 66–71.

29. Rawls, *Theory*, 109.

30. Rawls, *Political Liberalism*, 18–20.

31. Rawls, *Political Liberalism*, 30–32.

32. Rawls, *Political Liberalism*, 32–33.

33. Rawls, *Political Liberalism*, 33–34.

34. Rawls discusses the primary goods in *Theory*, 78–81, and in *Political Liberalism*, 178–182.

35. Rawls, *Political Liberalism*, 180. The second assumption here, that all citizens require the same primary goods in order to fulfill their higher-order interests, will be a

central focus of attention in my third section.   Sometimes Rawls treats this as a simplifying assumption, as at *Political Liberalism*, 180–81, n. 8.   At other times he defends it as an implication of his conception of equal citizenship, as at *Political Liberalism*, 330.

36. Rawls never provides a full-fledged argument for choosing this roster of primary goods over other possible lists, but he comes closest in *Theory*, 79–81. He also discusses the derivation of his list of basic rights and liberties in *Political Liberalism*, 291–294.

37. Rawls, *Political Liberalism*, 180.

38. Rawls, *Political Liberalism*, 29–35.

39. Rawls, *Political Liberalism*, 30–32.

40. In his sections entitled "Neither a Community nor an Association" and "Non-public Reasons," Rawls makes it abundantly clear that the only kinds of human collective groups which his theory admits are voluntary associations, societies, and morally arbitrary collections. See Rawls, *Political Liberalism*, 40–43, 220–222.

41. Rawls, *Political Liberalism*, 32–33.

42. The following discussion draws upon Iris Young's development of the concept of a social group in *Justice*, 42–44.

43. The image of social identity as being unlike a pop-bead necklace is taken from Elizabeth V. Spelman's introduction to Spelman, *Inessential Woman: Problems of Exclusion in Feminist Thought* (Boston: Beacon, 1988), 15.

44. This is the reason why Rawls designs the veil of ignorance so as to prevent the parties from knowing each other's sex, gender, race, ethnicity, etc. See Rawls, *Political Liberalism*, 24–25.

45. Rawls, *Political Liberalism*, 182–86. Rawls is responding to an objection originally developed by Amartya Sen in "Well-being, Agency, and Freedom: The Dewey Lectures, 1984," *Journal of Philosophy* 82 (1985), 169–221.

46. Will Kymlicka, *Liberalism, Community, and Culture* (Oxford: Clarendon, 1989), 164–166.

47. Will Kymlicka argues that Native Canadian cultures constitute such minority cultures within Canadian society in *Liberalism*, 140–205.

48. I do not mean to suggest that I accept Rawls's particular principles of justice as defining the bounds within which cultures must exist. Indeed, if Rawls's theory of justice is based on a theory of agency that is as individualistic as I have described it, then Rawls's principles of justice may pose problems for any culture requiring a strong communal life in order to flourish. It is at least questionable whether every such culture deserves to be condemned to the dustbin of history because it is insufficiently individualistic.

49. Kymlicka makes this point in *Liberalism*, 211.

50. This is known in the literature as the problem of expensive tastes. Will Kymlicka has a good discussion of John Rawls's and Ronald Dworkin's treatments of this problem in *Contemporary Political Philosophy: An Introduction* (Oxford: Clarendon, 1990), 73–76.

51. Rawls, *Political Liberalism*, 197–200.

52. Rawls, *Political Liberalism*, 330.

53. Rawls develops the Difference Principle in *Theory*, 60–65.

54. Kwame Anthony Appiah, *The Ethics of Identity* (Princeton: Princeton University Press, 2005), 120–127.

55. See Rawls, *Political Liberalism*, 35, 291.

56. Charles W. Mills, "'Heart' Attack: A Critique of Jorge Garcia's Volitional Account of Racism," *Journal of Ethics* 7 (2003), 51–57.

57. This type of attitude has historically been quite widespread among liberal political philosophers themselves. Perhaps the most famous expression of this form of racism is to be found in John Stuart Mill, *On Liberty*, ed. E. Rapaport (Indianapolis: Hackett, 1978), 9–10.

58. This phrase is taken from the title of Catharine MacKinnon's book, *Only Words* (Cambridge, Mass.: Harvard University Press, 1993).

59. Tommie Shelby, *We Who Are Dark: The Philosophical Foundations of Black Solidarity* (Cambridge, Mass.: Belknap Press of Harvard University Press, 2005), 53–57, 216–223.

60. Shelby, *We Who Are Dark*, 244–248.

61. Shelby, *We Who Are Dark*, 216–223.

62. See, for instance, Rawls, *Theory*, 386.

63. Rawls, *Theory*, 387.

64. Shelby, *We Who Are Dark*, 4–9.

Chapter Four
Autonomy, Individualism, and Social Justice

For over three centuries, liberal political philosophy has been one of the primary conceptual frameworks to which emancipatory movements in Europe and North America have appealed for justification. The commitments of liberals to individual autonomy, civil and political rights, and limited government have provided moral and political guidance to a wide variety of progressive social movements. The achievement of universal adult suffrage, formal equal opportunity for education and employment, and formal equality before the law regardless of race would hardly have been possible if members of progressive social movements pursuing these goals had not been able to appeal to liberal political values and concepts in order to justify their demands.

Nevertheless, philosophers of race and feminist political philosophers have long criticized mainstream liberal political theorists for failing to address directly certain forms of injustice directly related to race and gender.[1] In particular, feminist thinkers have argued that efforts of liberals to protect a private sphere of individual freedom from state interference have protected unjust treatment of women within the home by men from receiving political scrutiny and state sanction.[2] Their arguments often suggest that the distinction between public and private spheres is conceptually fundamental to liberal political philosophy, and that this distinction makes it impossible for liberals adequately to address issues of justice related to gender.

Will Kymlicka has risen to meet this feminist challenge by arguing that liberal political philosophers can, in fact, address the issues of justice related to gender by reformulating the conceptual framework of liberalism. In *Liberalism, Community, and Culture* and *Contemporary Political Philosophy*, Kymlicka develops a form of liberalism that is based on a revised version of the classical liberal ideal of autonomy.[3] Kymlicka's renewed conception of autonomy is based on the idea that human beings are by nature able to choose freely how to direct their own lives but that this ability can be effectively exercised only in certain material, political, and cultural circumstances. This idea leads Kymlicka to reinterpret the private-public distinction as a distinction between free choice and the circumstances required for free choice. Kymlicka takes pains to construct this distinction between free choice and circumstance without excluding gender relations and domestic affairs from political scrutiny, as earlier versions of the private-public distinction have done.[4] Kymlicka expresses the hope that the renovated form of liberalism will succeed in addressing sexism, racism, and other forms of injustice that are grounded in cultural contexts.[5]

Like most contemporary liberal political philosophers, Kymlicka views social justice as a matter of the fair distribution of income, wealth, rights, liberties, opportunities, and resources among the individual members of society. The various theories that share this basic view differ from one another primarily in how the fair distribution of these rights, liberties, opportunities, and resources among individuals are defined. Political philosophers who share this basic view that social justice is a matter of fair distribution may believe that social justice requires equal distribution among individuals or that it merely requires equitable distribution, but may permit strictly unequal distributions under certain circumstances.[6] Likewise, philosophers who share this basic view may believe that just distribution requires a certain end-state pattern once the distribution of resources is complete, or they may believe that just distribution merely requires that the process of arriving at a certain end-state pattern be fair, regardless of what that end-state pattern looks like.[7] Since the conflicts between these different views all presume the truth of the basic view about the nature of justice, the disagreements among these views all take place within what Iris Young has called the distributive paradigm of social justice.[8]

Like John Rawls, Kymlicka believes that social justice requires that society's scarce resources be divided fairly, although not necessarily absolutely equally, among individual members of society. And like Ronald Dworkin, Kymlicka believes that Dworkin's conception of equality of resources captures the nature of fair distribution of resources more adequately than Rawls's difference principle does.[9] Kymlicka's distinctive contribution to the contemporary debate about the nature of social justice is to reconnect recent liberal political theories that are formulated within the distributive paradigm of social justice with earlier, more classical forms of liberalism that emphasized autonomy conceived in terms of negative liberty, exemplified by the work of philosophers such as John Stuart Mill.[10] Kymlicka's hope is that with a properly broadened and strengthened conception of autonomy, liberalism can emerge as a force capable of combating racism and sexism and as the most theoretically adequate interpretation of the ideal of equality.[11]

Can the ideal of autonomy serve as the centerpiece of a progressive, emancipatory politics, as Kymlicka hopes? In order for us to respond affirmatively to this question, it must be possible to justify the demand to eliminate white supremacy, patriarchy, and other forms of domination and oppression by appealing to the ideal of autonomy. Whether an appeal to autonomy can justify this demand has been a hotly debated question among liberal and feminist political philosophers in recent years. Many feminist philosophers have denied that autonomy can play this role, but their denials have often been based on unnecessarily narrow definitions of autonomy as mere negative liberty, independence, or self-sufficiency. Some liberal political philosophers have responded by pointing out that while such narrow conceptions of autonomy may still be popular among right-wing libertarians, progressive liberals have long since developed richer conceptions involving not only the freedom to choose how to live but also the resources required to act on such choices.[12]

Other feminist philosophers have sought to redefine autonomy in such a way that it can serve as the centerpiece of an anti-patriarchal politics. They have pointed out that many of the demands for justice voiced by feminist and anti-racist activists seem to rely for their justification on an appeal to some ideal of personal freedom. Kymlicka thinks that such demands can and should be expressed in terms of demands for autonomy, and he hopes to find room within the conceptual framework of liberalism for the voicing of these demands.[13] If he is right, then progressive politics can fruitfully pursue autonomy as a central ideal within the context of the liberal conceptual framework.

We may distinguish between autonomy and personal freedom. Autonomy is a specific interpretation of the broad concept of personal freedom. Autonomy is usually understood to imply something like self-rule or self-determination, a freedom from constraints that are in some sense external. This is one familiar way, but just one way, to conceive of personal freedom. While there is a crucial role for an ideal of freedom to play in progressive politics, the specific concept of autonomy may not be able to play this role. While Kymlicka has made important, progressive changes to the concept of autonomy, the changes that he has made are consistent with the basic assumptions of the distributive paradigm of social justice and the conceptual framework of liberal political philosophy. These assumptions and this framework limit the range of forms of social injustice that welfare liberalism can address. Specifically, they pose conceptual obstacles to the elimination of some forms of injustice related to gender and race. As a result, feminist philosophers and philosophers of race should be wary of embracing Kymlicka's renewed conception of autonomy and the liberal theory of justice that accompanies it as a basis for building a political theory that can guide the way to the elimination of partiarchy and white supremacy.

1. Distributive Justice and the Conceptual Framework of Liberalism

Liberals value autonomy because they maintain that how the lives of people go should not be completely determined by the state, by other persons, or by the chance circumstances of their lives. Instead, people should be enabled to choose how to live for themselves and should have the opportunity to develop and carry out their own life plans. Liberals assign to the state the task of promoting the existence of social circumstances in which people can exercise this kind of autonomy.

Autonomy is a notoriously difficult goal for a state to promote, since liberals see state interference in the lives of people as one of the leading threats to autonomy. It is indeed impossible for a state to promote autonomy directly by coercive means, since an autonomous choice cannot, by definition, be coerced. A liberal state can only promote autonomy indirectly, by providing individuals with the means that they require in order to choose how to live and to act on those choices. This done, a state must allow people to decide freely how to use the means at their disposal. Welfare liberals operating within the distributive paradigm of social justice typically include among the means to autonomy not only civil and political liberties but also social resources such as income, wealth, and opportunities.

This account of the concept of autonomy and its role as a political ideal within liberalism should make clear that this concept is inextricably linked to two other key components of the liberal conceptual framework. One of them is the choice-circumstance distinction, which sets limits on what a liberal state may do in order to make autonomy achievable for persons. Liberals require a state to create the social circumstances that individuals need in order to exercise effective choice over how to live their lives. Liberals then forbid a state to interfere with freedom of choice for individuals by intervening in the lives of individuals any further than is required to ensure that the social circumstances exist.

Different versions of liberalism draw slightly different lines between the sanctioned state activity of creating the circumstances required for the exercise of autonomy, on the one hand, and the forbidden state activity of interfering with the autonomous choices of individuals, on the other. Some liberals see coercive taxation for the purpose of redistributing wealth, for instance, as a legitimate effort to provide all persons with the resources they require to exercise autonomy. Others see such a policy as illegitimate interference with the autonomous control by individuals of their property. But wherever the line is drawn, liberals must somehow distinguish normatively between the background circumstances within which individuals need to live if they are to be able to choose freely and the matters about which an individual ought to be free to choose.

The second component of the liberal conceptual scheme on which the liberal value of autonomy depends is an important assumption about the persons who are meant to exercise autonomy. This assumption concerns individualism and is the idea that for political purposes, persons should be treated as individuals, independent of their identification with any social group defined by characteristics such as race, sex, sexuality, culture, or religion. A liberal state need not treat persons as if they are or ought to be completely self-sufficient and independent of each other. Indeed, the just distribution of resources would not even be a concern if the resources were so plentiful that each individual could have as much as she needed without having to cooperate with others. A liberal state does, however, promote the conditions required for personal freedom of choice and action on the part of persons taken as individuals, rather than on the part of persons conceived as members of groups based on characteristics such as race, gender, or religion. Even liberals who stress the importance of memberships by individuals in cultural communities maintain that the members of such communities must be treated as individuals for political purposes.[14]

The reason why the promotion of autonomy as an ideal requires that persons be treated as individuals is that an autonomous person is a person who is in a position to choose for herself what her fundamental beliefs will be, what projects she will undertake, and what attachments and associations she will form with others. If a person's fundamental identity were inextricably tied to her membership in certain groups defined by race, gender, or class, such ties would seriously compromise these freedoms. Certain attachments, associations, and projects could be imposed upon her from the outside because they are in the interest of the groups to which she belongs. Such a person might be able to act freely in many respects, but overall it would not be accurate to say that she was choosing how her life would go "from the inside," in Kymlicka's phrase.[15]

The reason why it is practically significant for welfare liberals to treat persons as individuals can be seen in the rosters that welfare liberals offer of the social circumstances or means required for the exercise of autonomy. The means include material goods such as income and wealth, as well as abstract objects such as rights, liberties, and opportunities of various sorts, all of which can be controlled, used, exercised, or enjoyed by individuals. Since autonomy is the freedom of an individual to choose how to live and to act on such choices, the means required for the exercise of autonomy must be the sorts of things that can be controlled, used, exercised, or enjoyed by an individual. Many of the means required for the achievement of autonomy can only be provided through collective action by society as a whole. But all of the means can be possessed, controlled, used, exercised, or enjoyed by individuals. The commitment of many welfare liberals to this view of the means required for the exercise of autonomy expresses the fact many welfare liberal theories of justice currently operate within the distributive paradigm of social justice.

It might be thought that in defending a right to cultural membership on behalf of members of threatened minority cultures, Kymlicka has moved beyond the traditional liberal commitment to individualism. But Kymlicka takes care to avoid doing just this. First, he emphasizes that the rights he advocates granting to members of threatened minority cultures are universal rights that every individual has, regardless of cultural membership. Members of dominant cultures are simply in a position to take the rights for granted, and so do not need legal or political guarantees for them.[16] Second, he emphasizes that he is advocating granting minority rights not to minority cultures taken as wholes, but to the individuals who are members of the cultures. This enables him to treat the right to cultural membership as a kind of resource or primary good that can be distributed to individuals, and thus to deal with cultural membership while remaining within the distributive paradigm of social justice.[17] Taken together, these two steps allow Kymlicka to present his defense of minority cultural rights as a natural outgrowth of the liberal commitments to autonomy, individualism, and the choice-circumstance distinction, rather than as a rejection of any of these commitments.

Autonomy, individualism, and the choice-circumstance distinction form a conceptual triad at the core of liberal political philosophy. The meaning of each of these three concepts is intimately linked to that of each of the others. Autonomy specifies the goal that a liberal state is to promote. Individualism specifies the subject on whose behalf a liberal state is to promote this goal. The choice-circumstance distinction specifies what the state must do and what it must refrain from doing in order to promote that goal.

If the meaning of any of these concepts shifts, then the meaning of each of the others must shift along with it in order to maintain the integrity and stability of the conceptual framework. Libertarian political theorists, for instance, typically place material wealth on the choice side of the choice-circumstance distinction by maintaining that promoting autonomy entails permitting individuals to dispose of their material wealth as they please.[18] Welfare liberals shift material wealth over to the circumstance side of the choice-circumstance distinction by maintaining that having a fair share of material wealth is a prerequisite for exercising autonomy.[19] This shift in the choice-circumstance distinction forces correlated shifts in the meanings of "autonomy" and "individualism." Autonomy must shift from a mainly negative ideal of liberty to a more positive ideal involving the possession by individuals of the resources required to act on their free choices. Likewise, whereas libertarians conceive of an individual as a being whose freedom can be threatened only by coercion, welfare liberals shift to a conception of an individual as a being with material needs that must be met if he is to lead a fulfilling life.

The conceptual triad of autonomy, individualism, and the choice-circumstance distinction forms the basis for the definitions of social justice advocated by liberals. Liberal political theorists typically conceive of social justice as the existence of the social circumstances required for every individual to be able to exercise autonomy. Liberals then specify the creation and maintenance of social justice as the sole legitimate activity of a state. Exactly how social justice and the limited state are defined depends on the content of a particular liberal theorist's interpretations of the ideal of autonomy, the assumption of individualism, and the distinction between choice and circumstance.

The ideal of autonomy thus cannot be neatly detached from its conceptual underpinnings in liberal political philosophy. Any attempt to redefine autonomy within the conceptual framework of liberalism will require a redefinition of the concept of justice, the assumption of individualism, and the choice-circumstance distinction in order to maintain the integrity of the framework. The conceptual framework, together with the distributive paradigm of social justice in which it is normally articulated at present, provides a fair amount of flexibility and room for revision, but the flexibility and room are not infinite. An attempt to redefine one component of the conceptual framework by detaching it from one of the other components threatens to destabilize the entire framework. For this reason, a challenge to the assumption of individualism or the choice-circumstance distinction is itself a challenge to the liberal ideal of autonomy. If this assumption and this distinction cannot be maintained, then it becomes unclear how liberals can define social justice in terms of the social circumstances required for the exercise of autonomy. If we formulate an ideal of personal freedom without the assumption of individualism or the choice-circumstance distinction, then we move beyond the liberal conceptual framework altogether and begin to develop a new political theory.

2. Liberal Individualism and Controlling Images

An autonomy-centered approach to addressing white supremacy and patriarchy would have us maintain that neither race nor gender should be a bar to the achievement and exercise of autonomy. On a welfare liberal's account of the means to autonomy, this means that neither race nor gender should be an obstacle to the exercise of civil and political liberties or to the possession of a fair share of social resources such as income, wealth, and opportunities. Historically, liberals have appealed to the value of autonomy to denounce patriarchal and white supremacist practices such as the denial of political liberties to white women and to African-Americans and refusals by employers to hire white women and people of color.

This autonomy-centered approach allows us to focus on the effects of white supremacy and patriarchy rather than their causes. Among the causes of white supremacy and patriarchy are beliefs, ideas, and attitudes which tacitly or explicitly promote or reinforce the subordination of people of color to whites and the subordination of women to men. These white supremacist and patriarchal elements of our culture are usually assigned to the choice side of the choice-circumstance distinction, since they form part of the moral or religious world views of many people and are thus protected from state interference by the freedom of conscience. A liberal state can directly combat these cultural expressions of white supremacy and patriarchy by exposing children to the ideology of egalitarian individualism in compulsory public education and by setting an example in treating all people as morally equal individuals regardless of their race or gender. Such liberal policies do a fair amount of good, but there are some manifestations of white supremacy and patriarchy which they do not touch.

One of the leading manifestations of white supremacy and patriarchy in North American society is the power of whites and men of all races to force persons of color and women of all races to conform to their white supremacist or patriarchal expectations in order to find a stable, secure place in society. Social theorist Patricia Hill Collins argues that the subordinate racial and gender roles of African-American women are partly defined by what she calls controlling images of African-American women.[20] A controlling image is similar to a stereotype insofar as it is a demeaning, belittling image of the members of a certain social group. But whereas a stereotype simply misrepresents the behavior and attitudes of a group, often by glossing over the differences between the group's members, a controlling image defines a subordinate social role which group members are encouraged to fill by promises of rewards or threats of punishments. Controlling images shape the perceptions and expectations of dominant group members about members of subordinate groups, and they justify the use of social and economic power to force subordinate group members to fill the roles. Controlling images thus link discourses and ideas about race and sex to oppressive practices and institutions by justifying and reinforcing the operation of the practices and institutions. They take white supremacy and patriarchy out of the discursive realm of mere words and into the real world of sticks, stones, and broken bones.

The autonomy-centered approach to white supremacy and patriarchy does address some of the unjust effects caused by white supremacist and patriarchal controlling images. A liberal state is meant to ensure that people of color and women of all races are able to exercise their civil and political liberties freely, even if some controlling images depict them as lacking the rational faculties that would entitle them to such liberties. Welfare liberals also maintain that all people of color and all women are entitled to fair shares of social resources, even if the controlling images of welfare bums and welfare mothers are of persons who have brought poverty on themselves through laziness, irresponsibility, or immorality.[21] Moreover, many forms of welfare liberalism would have us sanction preferential hiring of members of previously excluded groups as a temporary, remedial measure to correct the vast imbalance of power and wealth between white, non-Latino men and all other members of society. Such programs operate in the face of powerful controlling images of members of the targeted groups as incompetent and undeserving.

An autonomy-centered approach to white supremacy and patriarchy cannot, however, root out the cause of these injustices, namely the controlling images themselves. An autonomy-centered approach cannot prevent white people from feeling fearful of and threatened by young African-American men, making it difficult or impossible for them to feel at ease in any public or private space that they share with young African-American men. Their feelings of fear and loathing, partly inspired by media images of African-American males as gang members, drug dealers, and pimps, contributes significantly to many of the injustices suffered by African-American men, including economic exploitation, unemployment, and impoverishment. Affirmative action by itself will not conquer the feelings or eliminate the resulting forms of injustice. Affirmative action may place whites more frequently in situations where they must interact with African-American men in the classroom or the workplace. Depending on the interactions, whites may be encouraged to overcome their prejudices or to entrench their prejudices more deeply. The controlling images of young African-American men and the fears and insecurities that the images arouse in whites must be addressed head-on if the interracial interaction made possible by affirmative action is to have its maximum benefit for race relations.

Patriarchal controlling images pose related problems for the autonomy-centered liberal approach. Women of all races struggle with the controlling images of the nurturing, self-sacrificing mother and the dragon lady as they seek to advance in professional fields. The images create a conflict between the demands of professional roles requiring aggressiveness, willfulness, and self-promotion and the demands of feminine gender roles requiring a passive, deferent, reserved attitude. Many professional women find that they are expected to fill both conflicting sets of roles at once in order to advance their careers. Fulfilling either role too completely often results in a woman being branded either as a dragon lady, on the one hand, or as lacking in leadership qualities or commitment to her career, on the other. When the definition of professional merit is contradictory for women in a way that it is not for men, affirmative action alone will not create gender balance in upper management or the boardroom. The conflicting roles and images themselves must be revised in order for women and men to have equal opportunity for professional advancement. Carrying out this revision requires addressing controlling images of women head-on.

Many liberals would concede that affirmative action alone or in combination with traditional liberal commitments to the defense of civil and political rights and the redistribution of wealth will not suffice to eliminate white supremacy and patriarchy, and would point to anti-white supremacist and anti-patriarchal education as supplying the rest of the solution. Educational programs certainly do have a role to play in achieving this goal, but the content and aims of the educational programs will matter a great deal. Liberal political philosophers have long stressed the positive effects of mandatory public education in inculcating the ideology of egalitarian individualism in the formative years of children. Such an educational program would involve educating people to believe that persons should be treated as individuals, whose race, sex, class, and sexuality are morally irrelevant to their unique, idiosyncratic identities. Liberals would encourage teaching children that controlling images are unjust because they injure persons by treating them as members of races, genders, classes, or sexual groups rather than as pure individuals, thereby violating their dignity as individuals.

Such a liberal program of anti-white supremacist, anti-patriarchal education is doomed to fail, however, because it fails to locate the harm of white supremacist and patriarchal controlling images correctly. Membership in a variety of social groups is an irreducible part of the identities of persons. We inevitably interact with each other partly on the basis of cultural images of the groups that we belong to. There is no prospect of creating a society of pure individuals, now or in the future. Therefore, the goal of encouraging people to interact with each other solely on the basis of their identity as individuals is impossible to achieve. That goal, however, is misplaced from the beginning. The harm of controlling images is not that they encourage people to interact with each other partly on the basis of group memberships. This, in itself, is harmless. The harm of controlling images lies in the power they give to members of some groups, especially white, non-Latino men, to dominate others, especially people of color and women of all races. Therefore, the liberal program of anti-white supremacist, anti-patriarchal education will not enable us to combat white supremacy and patriarchy successfully because it misrepresents the harm done by white supremacist and patriarchal controlling images.

Consider, for instance, the controlling image of the black rapist. The main harm of this powerful image is not that it encourages us to violate the individual dignity of African-American men by treating their status as African-Americans or men as important parts of their identity, or that it promotes the false generalization that all African-American men are prone to act in a sexually predatory way toward white women. A liberal program of anti-white supremacist education that suggested otherwise would be misleading. The main harm done by this image is that it gives white men and women the power to dominate and oppress African-American men on the grounds that they pose a threat of sexual violence to white women simply by virtue of being African-American men. An effective strategy of anti-white supremacist, anti-patriarchal education would show how this controlling image helps reinforce relationships of domination and oppression. Emphasizing the powerful cultural currency of this image and analyzing the social and cultural causes and political, economic, and psychological effects of its persistent power can help white and nonwhite students to understand the structure and force of white supremacy in contemporary American culture.

An educational program that would have us make a serious effort to carry out this task should have us examine carefully the social operations of power in constituting social groups and defining the identities of people in terms of their memberships in such groups. It should have us examine how some of the groups are positioned to dominate and oppress others, and how domination and oppression is expressed and reinforced culturally, socially, economically, and politically. It should have us study how the lives of people are shaped by their experiences of membership in oppressed and oppressing groups. Such an educational program would need to engage in what Robert Post and Anthony Appiah have called soul-making, that is, attempting to reshape dominant cultural images of social groups that limit the freedom of members of the groups in question.[22] An educational program that helped students to carry out this kind of analysis would need to be based on a conception of a person as something more than an individual whose core identity should not involve identification with any social groups defined along lines of race, gender, class, or sexuality. Such a conception of personhood would conflict directly with the liberal commitment to individualism, and an educational program based on such a conception could not consistently be carried out within the liberal conceptual framework.

Racial and gender images, attitudes, and ideas are so deeply ingrained in American culture that it is difficult to imagine that race or gender could ever fade away into social insignificance. But even if race or gender did come to be irrelevant to a person's social identity sometime in the distant future, human interactions would continue to be shaped by the social identities of other groups and their cultural images. It is unrealistic to expect identification with social groups ever to cease influencing social interactions. The group identifications that are most important to our social identities will undoubtedly shift and change over time, but it is fanciful to imagine that the importance of group identifications to social interaction will ever simply fade away. It is therefore unhelpful for public educators to teach that a society of pure individuals will someday arise in North America, or indeed that such a society already exists. We cannot wish controlling images out of existence. We must confront them. Until we eliminate white supremacist and patriarchal controlling images from our culture, along with the subordinate social roles they justify and reinforce, white men will remain dominant in all major spheres of society, and persons of color and women of all races will remain subordinate to them.

What is required to eliminate white supremacy and patriarchy, at least as a beginning, is that the members of subordinate racial groups and women gain the power to participate in determining their own social roles and the social conditions in which they live. Men and women of color must gain the power to articulate how racial subordination constrains their lives and causes them suffering. Women of all races must gain the power to articulate how oppressive gender roles limit their lives and force them to place the needs and desires of men before their own. Until members of subordinate racial groups and women are able to help determine their own social roles and the conditions in which they live, white supremacy, patriarchy, and other forms of domination will persist, no matter how rights, resources, and opportunities are distributed across society.

This process of uncovering, analyzing, and naming the social and cultural forces that shape our lives in various liberating and oppressive ways can only take place within a culture of social criticism. A culture of social criticism is a culture in which ideas, images, discourses, institutional structures, and traditions are taken seriously for their power to liberate or oppress. A culture of social criticism would have us concede that social power is always at work in our lives and stands to improve the life chances of some people and to worsen the life chances of others. It allows us to acknowledge that it is impossible for any member of society to attain a God's-eye perspective on the structure of the society. Thus the best we can do is to be as aware of the functioning of social power as possible and to take account of its effects as we engage in dialogue about the best means of limiting its harmful effects. The ultimate goal is not individual choice that is not unfairly constrained by social circumstances, as liberals would have it, but active participation in a social, cultural, and political struggle that encourages us to reconfigure existing power relations of domination and oppression in order to eliminate or reduce their harms as far as possible.

3. Beyond Liberal Individualism

A liberal committed to creating a non-white supremacist, non-patriarchal society in North America might accept the claims we have considered about empowerment and self-determination and wish to incorporate them into an autonomy-centered account of social justice. Kymlicka expresses optimism that liberalism can accommodate similar claims within an autonomy-centered account of social justice. He does not, however, show how this might be done, and it is not clear how it could be accomplished.[23] A culture that is free of white supremacist and patriarchal controlling images is not the sort of thing that an individual can possess, use, exercise, or enjoy on her own, independently of other individuals. A culture inherently involves relations between persons, and cannot be conceived in purely individualistic terms. For this reason, the creation of a non-white supremacist, non-patriarchal culture is a collective good that will not fit into the individualistic account of the means to autonomy of a welfare liberal who remains committed to the distributive paradigm of social justice.

The attempt to create a non-white supremacist, non-patriarchal culture thus places unbearable pressure on the assumption of individualism made by welfare liberals who operate within the distributive paradigm of social justice. This assumption views persons as beings who can achieve autonomy if provided with the proper kinds and amounts of resources. As long as welfare liberalism retains the assumption of individualism in this form and thus continues to be formulated within the distributive paradigm, its conceptual framework will remain too rigid to permit liberals to pursue the creation of a non-white supremacist, non-patriarchal culture as a social goal. As long as this is the case, liberals will be limited to treating the symptoms of white supremacy and patriarchy without addressing the underlying cultural causes of these forms of domination and oppression.

Welfare liberals thus face a choice between three alternatives that will probably strike many of them as unappealing. First, welfare liberals could remain securely within the distributive paradigm of social justice and continue to defend an assumption of individualism framed in terms of the idea of justice as equality of resources. Second, they could abandon the distributive paradigm of social justice in order to develop an autonomy-centered approach to social justice that is not constrained by the framework of the distributive paradigm. Finally, they could strike out on a post-liberal path by abandoning their traditional focus on autonomy and developing a conception of social justice that is centered on a broader conception of personal freedom. In the remainder of this chapter, I will examine each of these alternatives in turn.

The first alternative is that welfare liberals could remain securely within the distributive paradigm of social justice and continue to defend an assumption of individualism framed in terms of the idea of justice as equality of resources. However, this option would prevent welfare liberals from addressing the root causes of white supremacy and patriarchy. This result is unlikely to appeal to liberal theorists who sought to promote the expansion of civil and political rights and the more equitable distribution of social resources during the latter half of the twentieth century. For this reason, I will not address this first alternative further.

The second, more promising alternative, is that welfare liberals could abandon the distributive paradigm of social justice in order to develop an autonomy-centered approach to social justice that is not constrained by the framework of the distributive paradigm. Welfare liberals could thus rise to the challenge of addressing the cultural roots of white supremacy and patriarchy by reinterpreting the assumption of individualism and the choice-circumstance distinction in a way that does not assume that social justice is purely a matter of distributing resources fairly. This would require thinking of an individual not only as having material needs, but also as being embodied as a member of a specific race and a specific sex, and thus as having interests that are unavoidably tied up with the interests of other members of his or her race and sex.

For instance, an African-American male in the United States has an interest in the eradication of the controlling image of the black rapist from American culture. Since this is true whether or not he chooses to take on the eradication of this image as a personal project of his, this interest cannot be located on the choice side of the choice-circumstance distinction. But neither is the eradication of this image from American culture a matter of distributing any social resource more equitably among individual members of society. It may be a background circumstance that must exist in order for African-American men to achieve autonomy, but it is not the sort of background circumstance that can be conceived as a social resource in the context of the distributive paradigm of social justice. For this reason, welfare liberals cannot place it on the circumstance side of the choice-circumstance distinction as long as it operates within this paradigm. Both the nature of the individual and the character of the social circumstances that individuals require in order to choose freely must be reconceived in order to address the problem of controlling images within a welfare liberal conceptual framework.

Some self-avowed liberal political philosophers who take racial oppression to be a serious form of social injustice acknowledge the way that cultural phenomena such as controlling images create obstacles to personal development and human fulfillment for members of subordinate racial groups. For instance, Anthony Appiah argues that some kinds of projects, such as the resistance of the operation of white supremacist controlling images, may become important to a person simply because of the kind of person that they are, say, African-American instead of white American.[24] Appiah also recognizes that in any given period of time, some of the social identities that exist serve as parameters within which people are free to develop their own identities, while others serve as limitations on people's freedom to do the same.[25] Appiah's recognition that some social identities serve as limitations on people's freedom and self-development allows him to acknowledge that some people have an interest in the reshaping of their social identities. This interest cannot be understood as an interest in having a greater individual share of some social resource, and Appiah does not argue that it can be so understood.

Likewise, Tommie Shelby's seminal work on black solidarity is grounded in the position that all African-Americans have an interest in resisting and eliminating various forms of racial stigmatization that lead to racial discrimination against African-Americans, no matter whether or not they happen to have taken this on as a personal project.[26] The creation of a culture that is free of racial stigmatization may be a background circumstance that members of subordinate racial groups require in order to attain autonomy, but it is not the sort of background circumstance that can be created simply by redistributing social resources. Appiah and Shelby alike express their allegiance to the liberal tradition and to the specific value of autonomy.[27] Appiah and Shelby's express commitments aside, however, it is an open question whether their common goal of resisting racial oppression can actually be realized within the scope of a theory of justice that remains centered on the value of autonomy.

It is difficult to imagine how welfare liberals could revise their interpretation of the assumption of individualism in order to address the challenge of cultural background conditions for the attainment of personal freedom and still maintain the rest of the liberal conceptual framework intact. Liberals seek to make the attainment of autonomy possible for the individual who is at the heart of its concern and its conceptual framework. Autonomy has been conceived in many ways by different philosophers, but it has always retained some link to the core ideas of self-rule and independence. How far can liberals such as Appiah and Shelby go in imputing shared, unchosen interests in the attainment of collective goods to individuals while still maintaining that individuals are, in the most fundamental sense, capable of independence and self-rule?

The limits of this approach are most evident in the work of Appiah. While Appiah goes well beyond Rawls in acknowledging the importance of the kind of person one is to determining the kinds of projects that one can pursue, his freedom to explore this importance and its implications is limited by his commitment to a position that he calls ethical individualism, that is, the position that all rights claims must be justified on the basis of what the rights in question do for individuals, rather than social groups.[28] When examining, say, the effects of white supremacist controlling images on African-Americans, however, it is not clear that the interests of individual African-Americans can be neatly separated from the interests of African-Americans as a social group. As I have argued above, the eradication of white supremacist controlling images is a collective good of a sort that cannot easily be accommodated within the limits of Appiah's ethical individualism.

Shelby's work is subject to the same limitations, although the limitations are not as immediately apparent as they are in the case of Appiah. Shelby offers an extended argument for the claim that African-Americans ought to work together on a basis of black solidarity for the elimination from American culture of forms of racial stigmatization that have led to racial discrimination against African-Americans in the past and present.[29] Shelby's argument entails that African-Americans have a shared interest in the collective good of the creation of a non-white supremacist culture in the United States. Yet Shelby claims at the outset of his argument that he intends his argument to be completely consistent with the political liberalism of John Rawls, which, as I have argued above, is located squarely within the framework of the distributive paradigm of social justice and is subject to all of the limitations of that framework.[30] If my argument is sound, then Shelby needs to choose between his commitment to the claim that African-Americans have a shared interest in the creation of a non-white supremacist culture in the United States and his commitment to the political liberalism of John Rawls. He cannot consistently maintain both commitments at once.

If Appiah were to abandon his commitment to ethical individualism or if Shelby were to abandon his commitment to the political liberalism of John Rawls, then he might embrace the third and final alternative described above. That is, he could leave behind both the distributive paradigm of social justice and the individualistic ideal of autonomy and strike out on a clearly post-liberal path in order to pursue a broader ideal of personal freedom. It is worth noting that even if it is not possible to appeal to an ideal of autonomy in order to justify a demand that certain controlling images must be eliminated from American culture, we clearly must appeal to some ideal of personal freedom in order to support this demand for justice. White supremacist and patriarchal controlling images are objectionable because they unfairly constrain the freedom of members of subordinate social groups to help determine the social conditions in which they live, the social roles they fill, and how they choose to live out their lives in that social context. The next step is to find a less individualistic conception of a person that can serve as the basis for an ideal of personal freedom that can explain how controlling images unfairly constrain the freedom of people.

One political philosopher who has made strides toward developing a less individualistic conception of personal freedom while maintaining some continuity with the liberal tradition in political philosophy is Joseph Raz. Whereas Appiah retains a commitment to ethical individualism that I have argued is characteristic of autonomy-centered approaches to social justice, Raz is committed instead to what he calls the humanistic principle: "[T]he explanation and justification of the goodness or badness of anything derives ultimately from its contribution, actual or possible, to human life and its quality."[31] On Raz's view, humanism becomes a form of individualism only with the added assumption that any collective goods are valuable for human beings only instrumentally, and not intrinsically.[32] Within this humanistic framework, Raz argues for an ideal of autonomy that he understands as a collective good, rather than as an individual good. Raz sees autonomy as a collective good because it depends upon the availability of a wide variety of acceptable alternatives, such as various careers and forms of relationships, for persons to choose between.[33] In the absence of a wide variety of careers and forms of relationships for a person to choose between, Raz argues that it is meaningless to say that the person can determine her or his life autonomously. Since the availability of various careers and forms of relationships within a culture is a collective good, autonomy is also a collective good.

Since the analysis of liberalism that I have presented in this chapter ties the liberal value of autonomy inextricably to an assumption of individualism, I am tempted to say that the ideal that Raz advocates is not autonomy, but a broader ideal of personal freedom. As a result, I am inclined to see his political theory not as a form of liberalism, but as a post-liberal political theory that maintains some historical continuity with the liberal tradition while transforming some of its basic assumptions. It is probably fruitless, however, to quibble over terms. I will focus my evaluation of Raz's work instead on its potential to help women and members of subordinate racial groups to attain freedom from patriarchy and white supremacy, rather than on the question of whether such freedom should be called "autonomy" or something else.

The willingness of Raz to address autonomy or personal freedom as a collective good suggests that his political theory may have the potential to serve as a framework for combating white supremacy, patriarchy, and other forms of oppression. Raz does little, however, to explore this potential himself. A culture might afford people many different career options and forms of relationships (such as forms of committed romantic relationships) to choose from while many white supremacist and patriarchal controlling images continued to operate unchecked.[34] Nowhere does Raz address the obstacles that such controlling images may pose to the full development and exercise of personal freedom on the part of nonwhites and women of all races. The failure of Raz to address such obstacles does not, of course, entail that such obstacles cannot be addressed within the framework of his political theory. This work remains, nevertheless, for others to do.

One philosopher who has tried to do some of this work is Anthony Appiah. As Appiah's frequent positive citations of Raz suggest, Appiah is sympathetic to Raz's project of developing a form of liberalism that pursues an ideal of autonomy or personal freedom that is not constrained by the assumptions of the distributive paradigm of social justice.[35] Appiah does go beyond Raz, on the one hand, acknowledging that a person's ability to achieve autonomy may be limited not only by a lack of interesting career options and a shortage of forms of personal relationships, but also by social identities that limit personal development.[36] But Appiah also refrains from stretching the boundaries of the liberal tradition so far as Raz does, on the other hand, by declining to embrace Raz's understanding of autonomy as a collective good and accepting the constraints of the assumption of ethical individualism.[37] In order to explore the emancipatory potential of Raz's political theory fully, a philosopher would need to embrace both Raz's understanding of autonomy or personal freedom as a collective good and Appiah's understanding of the way that some social identities may pose obstacles to the development of autonomy or personal freedom. Since I am not committed to maintaining continuity with the liberal tradition in political philosophy, I will leave this exploration to others who are. I maintain, however, that whether this path is, as Raz claims, liberal or, as I maintain, post-liberal, it is the one path open to those who are committed to addressing white supremacy and patriarchy from a generally liberal vantage point.

Notes

1. Philosophers of race who criticize mainstream liberals include Howard McGary, *Race and Social Justice* (Malden, Mass.: Blackwell, 1999); Charles W. Mills, in *The Racial Contract* (Ithaca: Cornell University Press, 1997); and Lucius T. Outlaw, Jr., in *On Race and Philosophy* (New York: Routledge, 1996). Feminist philosophers who criticize mainstream liberals include Lorenne M. G. Clark, "Women and Locke: Who Owns the Apples in the Garden of Eden?" in *The Sexism of Social and Political Thought: Women and Reproduction from Plato to Nietzsche*, ed. L. Clark and L. Lange (Toronto: University of Toronto Press, 1979), 16–40; Alison Jaggar, *Feminist Politics and Human Nature* (Totowa, N.J.: Rowman & Allanheld, 1983); Susan Moller Okin, *Justice, Gender, and the Family* (New York: Basic Books, 1989); Okin, "*Political Liberalism*, Justice, and Gender," *Ethics* 105 (1994); Jennifer Ring, "Mill's *The Subjection of Women*: The Methodological Limits of Liberal Feminism," *Review of Politics* 47 (1985).

2. See Jean Bethke Elshtain, *Public Man, Private Woman: Women in Social and Political Thought* (Princeton, N.J.: Princeton University Press, 1981) and Carole Pateman, *The Sexual Contract* (Stanford, Calif.: Stanford University Press, 1988).

3. Will Kymlicka, *Liberalism, Community, and Culture* (Oxford: Oxford University Press, 1989), and Kymlicka, *Contemporary Political Philosophy: An Introduction* (Ox-

ford: Oxford University Press, 1990).

4. Kymlicka, *Contemporary Political Philosophy*, 250–262.

5. Kymlicka, *Contemporary Political Philosophy*, 246–247.

6. For the former view, see Kai Nielsen, *Equality and Liberty: A Defense of Radical Egalitarianism* (Totowa, N. J.: Rowman & Allanheld, 1985). For the latter, see Rawls, *A Theory of Justice*, rev. ed. (Cambridge, Mass.: Harvard University Press, 1999); Ronald Dworkin, "What is Equality? Part 1: Equality of Welfare," *Philosophy & Public Affairs* 10, no. 3 (1981), 185–246; and Dworkin, "What is Equality? Part 2: Equality of Resources," *Philosophy & Public Affairs* 10, no. 4, 283–345.

7. The former view is represented by Rawls, *A Theory of Justice*, and the latter by Robert Nozick, *Anarchy, State, and Utopia* (New York: Basic Books, 1974).

8. Iris Young, *Justice and the Politics of Difference* (Princeton, N.J.: Princeton University Press, 1990), 15–38.

9. Kymlicka, *Contemporary Political Philosophy*, 84–85.

10. Kymlicka, *Contemporary Political Philosophy*, 88.

11. Kymlicka, *Contemporary Political Philosophy*, 1–5.

12. See Kymlicka, *Liberalism, Community, and Culture* (Oxford: Oxford University Press, 1989), 14–17, and John Rawls, *Political Liberalism* (New York: Columbia University Press, 1993), xxix.

13. Kymlicka, *Contemporary Political Philosophy*, 246–47.

14. See Kymlicka, *Liberalism*, 237–242, and Kymlicka, "Rethinking the Family," *Philosophy and Public Affairs* 20 (1991): 93–97. See also Kwame Anthony Appiah, *The Ethics of Identity* (Princeton: Princeton University Press, 2005), 71–72, 267–272.

15. Kymlicka, *Liberalism*, 12, 53–58.

16. Kymlicka, *Liberalism*, 186–190.

17. Kymlicka, *Liberalism*, 199–200.

18. Kymlicka, *Contemporary Political Philosophy*, 145–151.

19. Kymlicka, *Contemporary Political Philosophy*, 76–90.

20. Patricia Hill Collins, *Black Feminist Thought: Knowledge, Consciousness, and the Politics of Empowerment* (Boston: Unwin Hyman, 1990), 67–68.

21. Collins, *Black Feminist Thought*, 76–77.

22. Robert Post et al., *Prejudicial Appearances: The Logic of American Antidiscrimination Law* (Durham: Duke University Press, 2001), and Appiah, *Ethics of Identity*, 195–199.

23. Kymlicka, *Contemporary Political Philosophy*, 85–90, 240–247.

24. Appiah, *Ethics of Identity*, 21–26.

25. Appiah, *Ethics of Identity*, 110–113.

26. Tommie Shelby, *We Who Are Dark: The Philosophical Foundations of Black Solidarity* (Cambridge, Mass.: Belknap Press of Harvard University Press, 2005), 149–154.

27. Appiah, *Ethics of Identity*, 36–58, 155–165; Shelby, *We Who are Dark*, 4–9, 149–154.

28. Appiah, *Ethics of Identity*, 71–72.

29. Shelby, *We Who are Dark*, 141–144, 149–154, 248–254.

30. Shelby, *We Who are Dark*, 4–9.

31. Joseph Raz, *The Morality of Freedom* (New York: Oxford University Press, 1986), 194.

32. Raz, *Morality of Freedom*, 198–199.

33. Raz, *Morality of Freedom*, 203–207.

34. Raz, *Morality of Freedom*, 372–378.

35. See, for instance, Appiah, *Ethics of Identity*, 26–32, 36–40, 79–83.
36. Appiah, *Ethics of Identity*, 110–113.
37. Appiah, *Ethics of Identity*, 71–72.

Chapter Five
Distributive Justice and
the Injustice of Hate Speech

In chapter one, I argued that political philosophy ought to focus on white supremacy rather than on racism in seeking to understand race-related injustice because the concept of white supremacy does a better job of revealing the causes of race-related injustice. I applied this general conclusion to a specific case of race-related injustice in chapter two by analyzing two killings of African-American men by white police officers in Omaha, Nebraska, arguing that the concept of white supremacy shed more light than did the concept of racism on the causes of the various forms of injustice that occurred in each police killing.

In chapter three, I argued that the leading contemporary liberal theory of justice, that advocated by the late John Rawls, is not capable of addressing some of the ways in which white supremacy creates obstacles to the moral development and human fulfillment of nonwhite persons. A key feature of Rawls's theory of justice that limits its ability to address such obstacles is its view that social justice amounts to the equitable distribution of resources among the citizens of a society. I argued in chapter four that other liberal theories that share this distributive view of social justice also share Rawls's inability to address the cultural roots of white supremacy. As an example of the cultural roots of white supremacy, I discussed the cultural forms that Patricia Hill Collins calls controlling images.

My argument has thus led us to the conclusion that if we are to address and undermine white supremacy, then we need to address, among other things, the existence and operation of white supremacist controlling images. This conclusion may raise some concerns in the reader's mind. How serious are the harms that white supremacist controlling images inflict on members of subordinate racial groups? Assuming for the sake of argument that the harms inflicted are relatively serious, what, if anything, can society or the state justifiably do to prevent or redress the harms? Again, assuming that society or the state can justifiably act either to prevent or to redress the harms, can it do so without making things worse overall?

These concerns arise in an especially poignant way for liberal political philosophers. Liberalism has a deep and abiding commitment to the freedom of thought and expression as the most fundamental liberty enjoyed by free people. If people lack the freedom to form and express their own opinions about how best to live, then they will not be truly free to explore how best to live. The liberal commitment to the fundamental status of the freedom of thought and expression requires a correlated commitment to the importance of tolerating the expression of thoughts that conflict with one's own, even thoughts that one deems to be distasteful or offensive. Freedom of thought and expression effectively will not be available to all unless everyone is willing to tolerate the expression of conflicting thoughts by others. Liberal political philosophers are therefore likely to be concerned that my discussion of the role of controlling images in supporting white supremacy likely overestimates the harm inflicted by the expression of such images, underestimates the harm that society may inadvertently cause through its efforts to prevent or redress such harm, and fails to provide adequate justification for political action, and especially coercive state intervention, designed to prevent or redress such harm.

I understand and appreciate the seriousness of the concerns expressed above. Nevertheless, I shall argue in this chapter that social sanctions against hate speech that expresses white supremacist controlling images are justified despite these concerns. I shall address the case of hate speech because I believe that the expression of white supremacist controlling images in the form of hate speech is one form of expression that is so harmful and so unjust that the full weight of society's coercive power ought to be used to prevent or redress it. Many other forms of the expression of white supremacist controlling images may be addressed adequately without using society's coercive power. Hate speech, however, is an exception to this general rule, or so I shall argue. My endorsement of the use of society's coercive power to address the harms of white supremacist hate speech will heighten the contrast between my own approach to the cultural roots of racial injustice and the approach taken by liberal political philosophers who endorse the distributive theories of social justice that I criticized in chapters three and four.

I will examine the roots of concerns about the dangers of social sanctions against speech in section one of this chapter by analyzing the classic liberal argument in favor of absolute freedom of thought and expression that is found in John Stuart Mill, *On Liberty*.[1] On the basis of this examination, I will formulate two Millian challenges to any argument that supports social sanctions against thought and expression in section two. I will formulate and defend a proposal for social sanctions against hate speech that expresses white supremacist controlling images in section three. In the fourth and concluding section of the chapter, I will argue that my proposal for social sanctions against hate speech meets both of the Millian challenges that will be raised in section two.

1. Mill on the Freedom of Thought and Expression

John Stuart Mill's basic premise in *On Liberty* is that freedom is a necessary condition for the fulfillment of "the permanent interests of man as a progressive being."[2] Mill's idea, developed more fully in his *Utilitarianism*, is that because we humans are capable of developing our faculties and because our ability to experience the richest forms of human happiness depends upon the full development of our faculties, it is in our interest to develop our faculties as fully as possible.[3] Therefore, since freedom is necessary for the full development of human faculties, freedom is necessary for human happiness.

Mill specifies the nature of the freedom he has in mind by saying, "The only freedom which deserves the name is that of pursuing our own good in our own way, so long as we do not deprive others of theirs or impede their efforts to attain it."[4] Mill maintains further that such freedom necessarily involves the freedom of thought and expression, the freedom of tastes and pursuits, and the freedom of association.[5] Of course, the assertion that these forms of freedom are necessary for human happiness must be established by argument. Mill offers an argument in support of the assertion that the freedom of thought and expression, in particular, is necessary for human happiness in the second chapter of *On Liberty*.[6]

Mill offers four distinct reasons for thinking that human happiness requires the freedom of thought and expression. First, if an opinion is thought to be false, it may nonetheless turn out to be true. In this case, the suppression of an apparently false opinion would amount to the suppression of the truth. Second, even if an opinion not only appears false but also really is false, the false opinion may nonetheless contain a portion of the truth that may be omitted by the generally accepted opinion. In this case, suppression of the false opinion would hinder the discovery of that portion of the truth. Third, even if an opinion is not merely partly but wholly false, expression of the false opinion may nonetheless serve to remind people of the reasons why the contrary opinion is true. In this case, suppression of the false opinion would hinder people from maintaining a lively awareness of the justification for believing the contrary opinion. Fourth, even if an opinion is wholly false, its expression may nonetheless serve to remind people of the true meaning of the contrary opinion. In this case, suppression of a false opinion might lead to confusion or misunderstanding about the meaning of the contrary opinion.[7]

Mill claims that the freedom that is justified by these four arguments amounts to "liberty of conscience in the most comprehensive sense, liberty of thought and feeling, absolute freedom of opinion and sentiment on all subjects, practical or speculative, scientific, moral, or theological."[8] But Mill concedes that there are limits to the sphere of individual freedom in general, although he maintains that the specific freedom of thought and expression is absolute. In a passage immediately prior to the one quoted above, Mill spells out what he sees as the proper limits of the sphere of liberty:

But there is a sphere of action in which society, as distinguished from the individual, has, if any, only an indirect interest: comprehending all that portion of a
person's life and conduct which affects only himself or, if it also affects others,
only with their free, voluntary, and undeceived consent and participation. When
I say only himself, I mean directly and in the first instance; for whatever affects
himself may affect others through himself: and the objection which may be
grounded on this contingency will receive consideration in the sequel. This,
then, is the appropriate region of human liberty.[9]

When a person's conduct does affect others "directly and in the first instance," Mill argues that society is justified in intervening in the person's conduct to prevent harm to others. This argument issues in Mill's famous harm
principle:

The object of this essay is to assert one very simple principle, as entitled to govern absolutely the dealings of society with the individual in the way of com-
pulsion and control, whether the means used be physical force in the form of
legal penalties or the moral coercion of public opinion. That principle is that the
sole end for which mankind are warranted, individually or collectively, in interfering with the liberty of action of any of their number is self-protection.[10]

Mill goes on to say that the fact that a person's actions will harm him is not
a sufficient justification for society to interfere with his actions by applying legal
or moral force. He lists various kinds of harm that one could do to oneself, and
says of them,

These are good reasons for remonstrating with him, or reasoning with him, or
persuading him, or entreating him, but not for compelling him or visiting him
with any evil in case he do otherwise. To justify that, the conduct from which it
is desired to deter him must be calculated to produce evil to someone else. The
only part of the conduct of anyone for which he is amenable to society is that
which concerns others. In the part which merely concerns himself, his independence is, of right, absolute. Over himself, over his own body and mind, the individual is sovereign.[11]

Thus, action which harms others falls outside the sphere of individual liberty in Mill's view. Presumably, if a person's expression of her opinion were to
harm others, then society would be justified in using physical or moral coercion
to prevent her from expressing her opinion or to punish her for doing so. Mill's
sweeping, absolute statements about the scope of the freedom of thought and
expression suggest, however, that Mill believed that a person's expression of her
opinions could not harm others and that coercive suppression of the freedom of
expression therefore would not be justified under any circumstances. Nevertheless, if it could be shown that a person's speech can, in fact, harm others, Mill's
own harm principle would require him to accept that society can justifiably suppress such speech with legal or moral coercion.

In addition to the harm principle, Mill accepts another limitation on the
sphere of individual freedom. Humans who have not "attained the capacity of

being guided to their own improvement by conviction or persuasion" can justifiably be coerced to refrain from acting contrary to their own self-interest.[12] Among those who have not developed this ability, Mill includes both children and "those backward states of society in which the race itself may be considered as in its nonage."[13] Mill suggests that the latter category may include at least the French during the medieval period and the residents of the Indian subcontinent during the early modern period.[14] Given Mill's lifelong involvement with the British colonial government of India, one may wonder whether Mill also thought that the inhabitants of contemporary India, as well as other nonwhites, still remained in their nonage.

Taken in the context of the passages quoted at length above, this qualification of the harm principle suggests that Mill presumes that the full possession of reason is a prerequisite for being entitled to the full sphere of individual freedom that he wants to protect. Persons who deserve to have their liberty respected are capable of receiving, considering, and acting upon rational criticism, and are capable of rationally criticizing others in return. Conversely, beings who are not capable of this do not deserve to have their liberty respected.

Finally, Mill seems to recognize one additional limitation on the sphere of liberty that is specific to the freedom of expression. At the end of chapter two of *On Liberty*, Mill discusses the question whether people ought to be restrained from expressing opinions intemperately. He points out that the intemperate expression of an opinion may not only be offensive but may also make those of a contrary mind reluctant to give voice to their own opinions.[15] This reluctance is, of course, concerning to Mill because he believes that people do not truly have freedom of thought about a subject unless they also have the freedom to express their thoughts about the subject.

Nevertheless, three considerations prevent Mill from advocating regulation of the manner in which opinions are expressed. First, it is obviously difficult to draw a fine, bright line between temperate and intemperate expression of opinion.[16] Second, intemperate expression of opinion is primarily a threat to the freedom of expression of those who hold minority opinions, who are typically fewer in number and thus less powerful than those who hold the majority opinion. Yet, it is generally the more numerous and more powerful adherents of the majority opinion who demand that their counterparts who adhere to minority opinions advocate them temperately.[17] Third, Mill asserts that

> [i]t is, however, obvious that law and authority have no business with restraining either [majority or minority opinions], while opinion ought, in every instance, to determine its verdict by the circumstances of the original case – condemning everyone, on whichever side of the argument he places himself, in whose mode of advocacy either want of candor, or malignity, bigotry, or intolerance of feeling manifest themselves[.][18]

Presumably, what makes it obvious to Mill that intemperate expression of opinions ought to be enforced by moral pressure rather than legal coercion is his conviction that thought and expression affect only the subject who thinks and expresses those thoughts, and do not threaten harm to others. If Mill could be convinced that some forms of expression can and do harm others, then his own harm principle would justify legal regulation to restrain individuals to express their views temperately.

2. Mill's Challenges to Sanctions against Hate Speech

Mill does not address in *On Liberty* the question whether white supremacist hate speech deserves the protection of the freedom of thought and expression. Most of Mill's examples of forms of expression in *On Liberty* are examples of expressions of religious or philosophical views that were held by a small minority of contemporary Europeans.[19] But it is clear from the text of *On Liberty* that Mill believes that the freedom of thought and expression is absolute. In general, Mill believes that a person ought to be free to pursue his own good in his own way until and unless that pursuit harms others. Mill also believes that the free expression of one's thoughts does not harm others, so he concludes that freedom of thought and expression should not be limited in any way under any circumstances.

I shall make the case in section 3 that hate speech that employs white supremacist controlling images may justifiably be subject to state regulation or other social sanction. I would like my argument to convince liberals who are otherwise sympathetic to Mill's absolutist position on freedom of thought and expression that it is reasonable to make an exception to such an absolutist position in order to permit social sanctions against white supremacist hate speech in the interest of creating racial justice. In order to convince this audience, my argument must meet two challenges based in Mill's position.

First, a liberal who is generally sympathetic to Mill's view of freedom will endorse the harm principle, which permits the state to limit individual freedom only in order to prevent one individual from harming others.[20] This principle will permit the state to regulate hate speech that involves white supremacist controlling images if and only if it can be demonstrated that someone was or will be harmed in some specific way by the speech. Thus, the first challenge to my position will be to demonstrate that white supremacist hate speech does cause harm and to articulate as clearly as possible the type and seriousness of harm that it causes. This is a reasonable demand to make on my argument, since any theorist, liberal or not, who advocates the regulation of white supremacist hate speech will advocate such regulation in the interest of preventing or remedying some harm to someone. Likewise, any theorist, liberal or not, who advocates social sanctions against white supremacist hate speech will want to articulate as clearly as possible the nature and extent of the harm to be prevented or remedied.

Second, a liberal who is sympathetic to Mill's concerns about the ripple effects of placing limitations on individual freedom of thought and expression will want to know how social sanctions against white supremacist hate speech that my position envisions will avoid chilling speech about race generally. This, too, is a reasonable demand to make of my argument, since a theorist who is committed to undermining the cultural roots of white supremacy will certainly want to avoid making people afraid to talk about race. If a general chill were cast across all speech about race while our current, extremely unjust, hierarchical racial order still exists in the US, then white supremacy would be permitted to continue unchallenged in the US. This would be an extremely undesirable outcome for anyone who is committed to overcoming white supremacy, an outcome to be avoided at almost any cost. Therefore, it is reasonable that my argument should be able to meet both the first and the second Millian challenges to any position that endorses social sanctions against hate speech.

3. Regulating White Supremacist Hate Speech

While definitions of racial hate speech vary somewhat, it is generally viewed as involving the expression of a message of racial inferiority in a manner that is persecutory, hateful, and degrading.[21] Examples of a few incidents of hate speech will help to flesh out this definition:

(1) African-American employees of Frito-Lay in Jackson, Mississippi, received racist notes and threats and found their cars spray-painted with the slogan "KKK."[22]

(2) Colleagues of an African-American FBI agent subjected him to racist taunts and pasted a picture of an ape over his child's photograph.[23]

(3) An African student at Smith College discovered a note slipped under her door that read, "African Nigger do you want some bananas? Go back to the Jungle."[24]

(4) A campus radio station at the University of Michigan broadcast a call from a student who joked, "Who are the most famous black women in history? Aunt Jemima and Mother Fucker."[25]

(5) Two white students at Stanford University defaced a poster of Ludwig van Beethoven by drawing over it a derogatory stereotypical black countenance, and hung up the poster on the door of an African-American student in a predominantly black dormitory.[26]

Some incidents of hate speech convey an explicit or implicit threat of violence. In case (1) above, the graffiti on the employees' cars carried the thinly veiled threat of racially motivated violence against the employees by their reference to the best known group of white racist vigilantes in the United States. Current US jurisprudence treats threats of racist violence as speech that is immune from criminal sanction under the protection of the first amendment to the US Constitution. Other liberal democracies, however, treat speech that threatens racial violence or incites racial hatred as unprotected speech that ought to be subject to criminal penalties.[27]

Threats of racist violence threaten to undermine the security of the members of the racial group at whom the threats are directed. Mill recognizes the importance of security to human beings in chapter five of his *Utilitarianism*, where he ranks security second only to food among the necessary conditions of leading a happy life.[28] Insofar as threats of racist violence undermine the security of nonwhites, they harm nonwhites. For this reason, Mill could easily justify imposing

legal sanctions on threats of racist violence under the harm principle that he defends in *On Liberty*. Such threats would constitute a relatively narrowly defined
exception to the otherwise absolute freedom of expression that he defends in *On
Liberty*. Mill's discussion of how competing rights claims are to be balanced
against one another in light of a comprehensive view of utility suggests how he
might make room for such a narrowly defined exception to the right to free expression.[29]

Other incidents of hate speech, such as (2) through (5) above, do not directly threaten individual members of nonwhite racial groups with white supremacist violence. Instead, they degrade, persecute, and express hatred of nonwhites
without threatening nonwhites with violence. For this reason, such forms of racial hate speech will not fall within the relatively narrowly defined exception to
Mill's absolute position on freedom of expression that is outlined above. If, as I
hope to show, such forms of white supremacist hate speech do cause harm to
nonwhites, then they will constitute a more significant exception to the freedom
of expression than the narrowly defined exception discussed above.

Incidents of white supremacist hate speech that degrade, persecute, and express hatred of nonwhites without threatening violence against a nonwhite
group, such as (2) through (5) above, normally operate by invoking a controlling
image of the targeted racial group, such as the Negro/ape, the black mammy,
Jezebel, or Sambo. Like threats of violence against nonwhites, they aim directly
at the racial group as a whole, and only indirectly at its individual members.
They aim to portray the entire racial group, and thus each of its members, as
hopelessly inferior or subhuman and thoroughly deserving of degradation, per-
secution, and hatred. The threat posed by this form of white supremacist speech
does not relate primarily to the personal safety of the individual members of a
race, but to the status of all members of the racial group as the full moral equals
of their fellow humans. White supremacist hate speech intends to create an environment in which the status of nonwhites as the full moral equals of whites is
questionable in the minds of whites and nonwhites alike.

The messages of racial inferiority expressed in cases (2) through (5) are not
thoughtful contributions to a rational debate about the relative moral standing of
different racial groups, but hateful expressions of a desire to degrade and persecute. In this connection it is important to distinguish arguments for the conclusion that certain nonwhite racial groups are morally or intellectually inferior to
whites, such as those offered by Richard J. Herrnstein and Charles Murray in
The Bell Curve, from examples of hate speech, such as those listed in (2)
through (5), above.[30] Arguments for the intellectual or moral inferiority of nonwhites, offensive as they may be, can and should be analyzed, evaluated, and
rebutted rationally. It would be unwise and dangerous to suppress such arguments for precisely the reasons offered by Mill in *On Liberty*.

White supremacist hate speech, by contrast, is not intended to elicit rational
evaluation of evidence, but to evoke feelings of inferiority and fear among nonwhites and feelings of superiority and contempt among whites. When it succeeds
in evoking such feelings, hate speech serves as a cultural support for white supremacy. It uses white supremacist controlling images to create a cultural envi-

ronment in which whites feel justified in enjoying undeserved racial privileges and nonwhites' confidence in their moral equality to whites is undermined. In this way, white supremacist hate speech harms nonwhites.

The feature of white supremacist controlling images that is crucial for understanding the harms that they cause to nonwhites is the connection between controlling images, on the one hand, and social sanctions for fulfilling or failing to fulfill the expectations of controlling images, on the other. It would not be so bad for a white student at Smith College to send an African-American student a note saying, "African Nigger do you want some bananas? Go back to the Jungle," if no social sanctions were attached to being viewed as a Negro/ape.[31] In the real world of contemporary American racial politics, however, being viewed as a Negro/ape means that you are viewed as lacking the cultivation and intelligence required to belong to the student body of an elite, predominately white, American liberal arts college. For this reason, you are viewed as a trespasser on territory properly belonging to cultivated, intelligent whites.

Worse, the lack of cultivation and intelligence attributed may mean that you will be treated as a subhuman Negro/ape grotesquely posing as a human being, and therefore as deserving the moral contempt and disgust of your white superiors. Perhaps you are one of the barbarians of whom Mill spoke in *On Liberty*, who are not entitled to a full and equal complement of rights and liberties because you are incapable of rational self-direction and can benefit only from benevolent despotism.[32] For a member of a subordinate racial group that is distinctly outnumbered on the campus of an elite, predominately white American liberal arts college, such social sanctions threaten to undermine the confidence of group members in their equal membership in the student body and their equal moral standing with their white peers. They also threaten to create a campus environment in which the equal status of nonwhites as students and moral persons becomes questionable in the eyes of white students.

White supremacist controlling images can make it difficult for nonwhites to conceive of themselves as full moral persons who have permanent interests as progressive beings and who have the moral dignity, which Mill sees as deriving from the capacity to experience high-quality pleasures that appeal not only to the senses but also to the intellect.[33] When controlling images have this effect, they harm the members of nonwhite racial groups who are the target of the images. When white supremacist controlling images are expressed in the context of an argument that is offered as evidence in support of a claim that some nonwhite racial group is intellectually or morally inferior to whites, then it is normally possible to meet argument with counterargument and evidence with critical examination of evidence, just as Mill envisaged. But when white supremacist controlling images are expressed in messages that are plainly intended not to persuade, but to express hate, to degrade, and to persecute, then offering counterarguments or critiques is not an option. The only available means to avoid the harm done by such messages are to discourage, punish, or, in extreme cases, suppress their expression.

State punishment or suppression of hate speech will, of course, involve the direct use of coercive force against the speaker. For this reason, liberals may prefer to address the harms of white supremacist hate speech through social persuasion to discourage hate speech rather than through state coercion to punish or suppress it. Perhaps the most subtle form of social persuasion for this purpose would be state-sponsored anti-white supremacist education. There is much to be said in favor of such a program, and I say some of it in chapter three. Three qualifications must, however, be kept in mind. First, any state-sponsored program that depends upon taxation of the public for its funding is indirectly, if not directly, coercive. After all, the legal requirement that citizens should pay taxes depends for its enforcement upon the coercive power of the state. If there were no threat of coercive power to support the requirement to pay taxes, then precious little tax revenue would be collected, and state programs funded by tax dollars would wither away.

Second, a state-sponsored program of anti-white supremacist education may be an effective means of discouraging white supremacist hate speech, but it is a means that is not available to a liberal political theorist who operates within the distributive paradigm that I discussed in chapter four. For in order to be effective in combating white supremacist hate speech, anti-white supremacist education needs to address the functioning and the power of white supremacist controlling images. This would mean educating students about how such images reinforce racial oppression and thereby harm subordinate racial groups as groups, and not primarily as individuals. To teach students to understand racism in this way thus amounts to demonstrating to them why the fundamental assumptions of the distributive paradigm are false. This, in turn, would undermine public acceptance of liberal political theories that operate within the distributive paradigm. For this reason, liberal political theorists cannot consistently appeal to anti-white supremacist education as a means of discouraging white supremacist hate speech.

Third, any state-sponsored program of anti-white supremacist education can be effective in discouraging white supremacist hate speech only if the educational program takes seriously the harm that can be done by such hate speech. But taking the harm of hate speech seriously requires society to be willing to punish such speech on the grounds that it has harmed the members of a nonwhite racial group or, in extreme cases, to suppress such speech before it can harm its intended victims. In the absence of society's willingness to punish or suppress white supremacist hate speech, it would be hard for the audience of an anti-white supremacist education program to credit the idea that the state sees the expression of white supremacist controlling images as harmful. Therefore, a state-sponsored program of anti-white supremacist education may be an important complement to coercive measures taken by the state against white supremacist hate speech, but it cannot be a replacement for such coercive measures. No one should be deceived into thinking that anti-white supremacist public education can serve as a detour around state action against white supremacist hate speech through the criminal law.

It is important to understand clearly the nature of the harm caused by white supremacist hate speech. Some critical race theorists have argued for the regulation of white supremacist hate speech on the grounds that it does emotional harms to its targets.[34] They are correct in noting that white supremacist hate speech has serious psychological consequences for its individual targets, making them feel dejected, worthless, and powerless in many cases. But they are incorrect in thinking that these emotional harms are the reason why hate speech should be regulated. White supremacist hate speech should be regulated because it helps to create, reinforce, and maintain white supremacy. It frequently does so by invoking white supremacist controlling images, those crystallizations of widespread cultural ideas about the inferiority of various nonwhite racial groups. The individual targets of white supremacist hate speech are made to feel the way they do because being targeted by hate speech amounts to being hit full force with your own culture's devaluation of you and all people like you. Hate speech brings the fact of white supremacy home, reinforcing and maintaining it. The emotional side effects of white supremacist hate speech are simply consequences of this fact.

White supremacist hate speech should be punished or suppressed because of its role in creating and sustaining white supremacy, even if it did not have any harmful emotional effects at all. One can easily imagine instances of hate speech that target tough-skinned individuals who do not feel deeply wounded emotionally by what is said to them. It may nonetheless be the case, however, that the incident may have the overall effect of contributing to white supremacy, and the targeted individuals may even be aware of this. In such a case, the act of hate speech is clearly harmful and should be subject to social sanctions, despite its lack of devastating emotional effects for its particular target.

Again, one can easily imagine instances of speech that express a message of racial inferiority in a hateful, degrading, and persecutory manner that causes the targeted individual to endure great emotional suffering. If, however, the speech in question does not contribute to the oppression of the targeted individual's racial group, perhaps because that group has not been historically oppressed, then I see no reason to punish or suppress it as hate speech. It might be subject to prosecution as a form of slander or another kind of verbal assault, but the category of hate speech does not apply unless the speech is oppressive.

4. Meeting Mill's Challenges

In section three, I argued that hate speech that expresses white supremacist controlling images seriously harms members of the nonwhite racial groups that are the targets of the hate speech, and that society is therefore obliged to impose sanctions against white supremacist hate speech in order to discourage, punish, or, in extreme cases, suppress its expression. I turn now to the question of whether the position that I defend in section three can meet the challenges that were raised in section two from the perspective of Mill's absolutist stance in defense of free speech.

The first Millian challenge to any position that advocates social sanctions against hate speech is that hate speech, like any other form of speech, is an expression of opinion that does not harm anyone, and it ought therefore to be immune to state regulation and social sanction. In section three, I noted that white supremacist hate speech is an expression of a message of racial inferiority that is not intended to persuade its target audience to adopt a certain opinion or viewpoint, but to persecute, degrade, and express hatred toward its target audience.[35] I then argued that white supremacist hate speech helps to create and maintain a cultural environment where whites treat nonwhites as their moral inferiors. White supremacist hate speech can encourage whites to feel justified in enjoying unfair privileges on the basis of their racial identity and can discourage nonwhites from viewing themselves as the moral equals of whites. Thus, white supremacist hate speech can serve as a cultural support for the existence of white supremacy, thereby causing serious harm to nonwhite racial groups. White supremacist hate speech therefore does harm nonwhites and, contra Mill, ought not to be immune to social sanctions.

The second Millian challenge to any position that advocates the regulation of white supremacist hate speech is that the regulation of white supremacist hate speech risks causing a chilling effect on speech in general, and speech about race in particular, and that this risk outweighs any potential benefits to be gained by the regulation of white supremacist hate speech. As I conceded above in section two, the risk of chilling speech about race by regulating white supremacist hate speech is real and serious. Three measures can be taken to minimize this risk.

The first measure is to determine carefully the intent of a speaker who expresses a message of racial inferiority. Speech expressing a message of racial inferiority that intends to persecute, degrade, and express hatred of its target audience should be treated as hate speech and should subjected to social sanctions as a result. Speech expressing a message of racial inferiority that intends to persuade its target audience to adopt a certain viewpoint or opinion should not. Discerning the intent of a speaker may prove difficult in practice, but many distinctions in criminal law, such as the distinction between murder and manslaughter, depend crucially on discerning the intent of an agent. In this respect, then, imposing sanctions against hate speech will be neither more nor less difficult than imposing sanctions against various forms of criminal behavior.

Moreover, in many cases, the intent of the speaker is plain. On the one hand, when G. W. F. Hegel argues that Africa has no history, he is clearly expressing a message of racial inferiority that is intended to persuade his audience to share his opinion of persons of African descent.[36] This is persuasive speech, and it can and should be rebutted by argument, not regulated by the state. On the other hand, when a caller to a talk radio show says that the most famous women in African-American history are Aunt Jemima and Mother Fucker, he or she is clearly expressing a message of racial inferiority that is intended to persecute, degrade, and express hatred toward African-American women. This is not an argument but hate speech. It cannot be rebutted effectively by argument, so it should be subject to social sanctions.

The second measure that can be taken to minimize the risk of chilling speech about race is to punish most acts of white supremacist hate speech only through what Mill calls the "exercise of the moral authority of public opinion," reserving legal regulation and state-enforced sanctions only for the most harmful instances of such speech.[37] Public opinion can mobilized effectively to punish instances of white supremacist hate speech, as was demonstrated by the public outcry that led to the firing by NBC of talk-show host Don Imus in the wake of his racially disparaging remarks in 2007 about the Rutgers University women's basketball team.[38] Mill famously expressed grave reservations that the exercise of the moral authority of public opinion could lead to a tyranny of the majority over the minority.[39] Nonetheless, so long as care is taken to distinguish between persuasive speech and hate speech in the manner suggested above, the exercise of the power of public opinion against instances of hate speech can provide society with a effective middle path between taking no action against hate speech, on the one hand, and bringing the full coercive power of the state to bear on hate speech through the application of the civil or the criminal law.

The third measure that can be taken to minimize the risk of chilling speech about race is to avoid suppressing white supremacist hate speech, as opposed to discouraging or punishing it, except in extreme cases. Jurisprudence concerning the first amendment to the US Constitution widely recognizes that exercising prior restraint over the expression of speech before it is expressed is a more serious and risky form of regulation of speech than punishment of speech that has already been expressed through, for instance, prosecution of charges of libel or slander.[40] The exercise of prior restraint is viewed as a most serious form of interference because it precludes the expression of the speech altogether. It is also especially risky because its justification depends on speculation about the harm that is likely to result from speech that has not yet been expressed, rather than an evaluation of harm that expressed speech has already caused. Moreover, prior restraint encourages self-censorship, and anything that encourages self-censorship risks causing a chilling effect on speech. For these reasons, the state should regulate white supremacist hate speech by suppressing it only in extreme cases, where the likely harm to nonwhites is expected to be severe and where this expectation is well-supported by evidence.

The regulation of white supremacist hate speech is a notoriously tricky issue because of the risk of regulating or simply chilling speech that should remain protected by the freedom of expression. Mari J. Matsuda proposes some guidelines that are a reasonable place to begin, and I will modify them only slightly to conform to the line of argument that I have adopted here. An instance of speech should be regulated as white supremacist hate speech only if: (1) the message expressed is one of racial inferiority, especially one that invokes a white supremacist controlling image; (2) the message expressed helps to maintain or reinforce white supremacy; and (3) the message is persecutory, hateful, and degrading.[41]

These three identifying conditions for white supremacist hate speech are not framed in the precise way that would be necessary if they were to become the basis of legislation. Framing legislation is, however, a task best left to lawyers, not philosophers.[42] In any case, the conditions above do specify the basic range of speech that I have in mind, and the underlying justification for regulating that range of speech, namely, to undermine and eliminate white supremacist controlling images and, ultimately, white supremacy itself. These should be goals for a state that is committed to the elimination of white supremacy.

The proposal that I make here obviously will not satisfy those who are interested in the tricky legal details of how to impose social sanctions against white supremacist hate speech without unintentionally causing all sorts of adverse effects. I concede that the devil is in the details with respect to this sort of social action, but I defer to those better qualified than myself to work out the details. One special concern is the possibility that social sanctions against hate speech will, if not carefully framed, be turned against the very subordinate racial groups that they are intended to help. An analogous difficulty arose when Canadian anti-pornography legislation, which was strongly advocated by a variety of feminist groups, was used to prosecute a gay and lesbian bookstore before the ink was dry on the law books.[43] I do not, however, see any reason to view these practical difficulties as insurmountable. Indeed, given the severity of the harms that are caused by white supremacist hate speech, every effort should be made to overcome them.

I hope that the responses to the two Millian challenges developed above will persuade liberal political theorists who are sympathetic to Mill's absolute position on freedom of speech to consider making an exception to this position in the case of white supremacist hate speech. I have argued that by the lights of Mill's own conception of liberty, the harms that white supremacist hate speech causes to nonwhites are serious enough to warrant regulation of such speech in the interest of undermining and ultimately eliminating white supremacy. For this reason, Mill and like-minded liberals have good reason to endorse the regulation of white supremacist hate speech on the basis of their own theoretical principles.

It is worth noting, however, that liberal political theorists who, unlike Mill, operate within the distributive paradigm cannot endorse the regulation of white supremacist hate speech in order to promote the goal of eliminating white supremacy. As I argued in chapter four, the elimination of white supremacy is not a good that an individual can possess, use, exercise, or enjoy on his or her own, so it cannot be treated as a good to be distributed to individuals. Consequently, political theories operating within the distributive paradigm cannot endorse state pursuit of the goal of eliminating white supremacy. In this way, my endorsement of the regulation of white supremacist hate speech marks a significant practical departure from liberal political theories that do operate within the distributive paradigm. This practical departure illustrates the significance of the theoretical critique of liberal political theories that operate within the distributive paradigm, which I developed in chapter four.

Notes

1. John Stuart Mill, *On Liberty*, edited by Elizabeth Rapaport (Indianapolis: Hackett, 1978).

2. Mill, *On Liberty*, 10; see also 4–5.

3. John Stuart Mill, *Utilitarianism*, second ed., edited by George Sher (Indianapolis: Hackett, 2001), 9–10.

4. Mill, *On Liberty*, 12.

5. Mill, *On Liberty*, 12.

6. Mill, *On Liberty*, 15–52.

7. Mill, *On Liberty*, 50.

8. Mill, *On Liberty*, 11.

9. Mill, *On Liberty*, 11.

10. Mill, *On Liberty*, 9.

11. Mill, *On Liberty*, 11.

12. Mill, *On Liberty*, 10.

13. Mill, *On Liberty*, 11.

14. Mill, *On Liberty*, 10.

15. Mill, *On Liberty*, 51.

16. Mill, *On Liberty*, 50–51.

17. Mill, *On Liberty*, 51.

18. Mill, *On Liberty*, 52.

19. See, for instance, Mill, *On Liberty*, 28–33, 39–41.

20. Mill, *On Liberty*, 9.

21. These are two of the three criteria for identifying hate speech that are developed by Mari J. Matsuda in "Public Response to Racist Speech: Considering the Victim's Story," in *Words that Wound: Critical Race Theory, Assaultive Speech, and the First Amendment*, ed. M. J. Matsuda et al. (Boulder: Westview, 1993), 36.

22. Matsuda, "Public Response," 21.

23. Matsuda, "Public Response," 21.

24. Charles R. Lawrence III, "If He Hollers, Let Him Go: Regulating Racist Speech on Campus," in Matsuda et al., eds., *Words*, 54.

25. Lawrence, "If He Hollers," 54.

26. Lawrence, "If He Hollers," 55.

27. See Charles Lewis Nier III, "Racial Hatred: A Comparative Analysis of the Hate Crime Laws of the United States and Germany," *Dickinson Journal of International Law* 13, no. 2 (Winter 1995), 259–67.

28. Mill, *Utilitarianism*, 54.

29. Mill, *Utilitarianism*, 55–59.

30. Rational (albeit fallacious) arguments for the moral or intellectual inferiority of nonwhites to whites would include, for example, the arguments made in Richard J. Herrnstein & Charles Murray, *The Bell Curve: Intelligence and Class Structure in American Life* (New York: Free Press, 1994).

31. Lawrence, "If He Hollers," 54.

32. Mill, *On Liberty*, 10.

33. See Mill, *On Liberty*, 10 and *Utilitarianism*, 9.

34. See, for instance, Richard Delgado, "Words that Wound: A Tort Action for Racial Insults, Epithets, and Name Calling," in Matsuda et al., eds., *Words*, 90–96; Lawrence, 72–76.

35. See Matsuda, "Public Response," 36.

36. G. W. F. Hegel, *Lectures on the Philosophy of World History*, trans. H. Nisbet (New York: Cambridge University Press, 1975), 174–76.

37. Mill, *On Liberty*, 83.

38. My thanks to Patrick Murray for helping me to see this point.

39. Mill, *On Liberty*, 4–5.

40. See, for instance, Daniel A. Farber, *The First Amendment*, second ed. (New York: Foundation Press, 2003), 46–49.

41. See Matsuda, "Public Response," 36.

42. Charles R. Lawrence III makes some interesting remarks about universities' failure to obtain qualified legal assistance in framing regulations of hate speech in Lawrence, "If He Hollers," 83–84.

43. See Janine Fuller et al., *Restricted Entry: Censorship on Trial* (Vancouver: Press Gang, 1995).

Chapter Six
After the Buses Stop Running:
Distributive Justice or Dialogue?

I have argued in chapters three and four that political theories that conceive of justice in exclusively distributive terms are not able to address the full range of forms of injustice that are related to white supremacy. They may be able to address some of the symptoms of white supremacy, such as poverty and discrimination, but they cannot address the power relations of domination and oppression that are the root causes of the symptoms. So long as the root causes of white supremacy remain at work in North American society, the symptoms will continue to recur unabated.

Advocates of theories of justice that operate within what I have called the distributive paradigm of social justice might reasonably respond to my critique with a challenge to suggest a superior alternative theory of justice that does not conceive of social justice in purely distributive terms. Some political philosophers have argued that a dialogical theory of justice is the best alternative to a distributive theory of justice.[1] On such a view, the focus of a theory of justice should shift away from the redistribution of social resources and toward the creation of social conditions in which an open, inclusive, and equitable social dialogue about matters of justice can take place. I am sympathetic to this view, and have argued in support of it in other contexts.[2] The present context does not permit sufficient space for the development and defense of a full-blown dialogical theory of justice. Nevertheless, it would be helpful to offer at least the beginning of an explanation of how a concern for social and political dialogue can enrich our thinking about social justice.

My aim in this chapter is to show how a dialogical theory of social justice can improve upon a distributive theory of social justice by supplementing such a distributive theory. I seek to answer the following question: if we were to hold up side-by-side a society where the distribution of resources was ideally just and another society in which the conditions required for an open, inclusive, and equitable social dialogue existed, in what way would the latter be manifestly superior to the former? I take it as granted that distributive justice, conceived in a relatively egalitarian manner, would necessarily exist in the latter society, since great disparities of material resources among participants in dialogue would certainly make the dialogue inequitable. So, we are not comparing a society with just distribution of resources to a society with unjust distribution of resources. But what exactly does the existence of open, inclusive, and equitable social dialogue about matters of justice add to a society where distributive justice exists?

The dialogical view of social justice is partly procedural, since it maintains that better conclusions about what justice requires of a given society will be achieved through an open, inclusive, and equitable dialogue among its members than by any other means. But a dialogical theory of justice must also be partly substantive, because it implies that justice specifically requires the creation of an open, inclusive, and equitable social dialogue and whatever material preconditions such a dialogue requires.

In this chapter, I argue that the existence of an open, inclusive, equitable dialogue about what justice demands of our society here and now is both an intrinsic part of any complete account of social justice and a necessary precondition for the existence of distributive justice. I argue that the existence of such a dialogue is necessary because society cannot effectively determine what justice requires of it without the existence of such a dialogue. In effect, I am arguing that social justice, including but not limited to distributive justice, cannot be achieved outside the context of participatory democracy, in which all members of society, even the most subordinate and marginalized, have an equitable opportunity to speak and be heard.

The dialogical view of social justice is often defended by theoretically examining a hypothetical case in which an open, inclusive, equitable dialogue is conducted under idealized, counterfactual circumstances. I find it unlikely, however, that such circumstances will be achieved anytime soon, so I consider it fruitless to argue that if they were achieved, then we could determine more accurately what social justice requires, in terms of the distribution of goods or anything else. If the dialogical view of social justice is to be of any practical political benefit to us, it must be able to help us determine how to take our society as it is and transform it into a more just society under actual, not hypothetical conditions. In order to see how a dialogical view of justice can help us with this task, I propose to examine a case study taken from contemporary US society.

The late 1990s and the first decade of the twenty-first century marked the end, for practical purposes, of the project of integrating public primary and secondary schools as a means to achieving racial justice in the United States due to shifts in American jurisprudence. Public school districts in urban centers across the United States dealt with the end of public school integration in a variety of ways. In the case I propose to examine, an election campaign about a local education bond issue in the city where I live, namely, Omaha, Nebraska, was contested in terms that model the debate between distributive and dialogical conceptions of justice. In May 1999, voters in the Omaha Public School District (OPS) narrowly approved a $254 million bond issue, the largest in Nebraska history. The 1999 OPS Bond Issue provided for an end to twenty-two years of desegregation busing in Omaha schools and major funding for capital and personnel improvements to schools across the district. Eighty-three percent of the funds from the bond issue was dedicated to the repair and renovation of aging school buildings, located primarily in predominately African-American north Omaha and predominately Latino South Omaha, and to the construction of a handful of new buildings in growing suburban areas in predominately white west Omaha.

The first section of this chapter analyzes the political and legal context in which the 1999 OPS bond issue was proposed and approved. I argue in section two that the 1999 OPS bond issue marked a shift from an ideal of social justice centered on integration toward another ideal of justice centered on fair distribution of resources. I indicate some of the limits of this distributive conception of justice in section three, from both a theoretical and a practical point of view. I argue that distributive justice must be carried out in a context of participatory democracy in order to achieve social justice in public education in present-day Omaha. Finally, I conclude with some remarks in section four about the broader philosophical implications of this case study.

1. The 1999 Omaha Public Schools Bond Issue Election

The decision by the OPS Board of Education to seek to end desegregation busing within the district was made in the context of national trends away from pursuit of the goals of integration and racial justice in jurisprudence, politics, and society at large. During the final three decades of the twentieth century, desegregation busing in urban US school districts was one of the most visible governmental efforts to undo the effects of centuries of *de jure* and *de facto* segregation in US society. Since the US Supreme Court required the School District of Charlotte-Mecklenburg, North Carolina, to implement a desegregation busing program in 1971, many urban school districts have introduced desegregation busing either involuntarily, under a judicial desegregation decree, or voluntarily, often in anticipation of a successful lawsuit and a resulting court order. As twelve years' worth of judges appointed to the federal bench by Presidents Ronald Reagan and George H. W. Bush rose through the ranks, it became easier for districts to end desegregation busing if they wish to and harder for them to continue busing even if they want to. This was the result of three related trends in US jurisprudence.

First, in the early 1990s, the Supreme Court weakened the standard that school districts operating under desegregation decrees need to meet in order to end court supervision of their operations. In *Board of Education of Oklahoma City v. Dowell* (1991) the Court allowed a desegregation decree to be partially removed, ending court supervision of those areas of operations in which unitary status, or integration, had been achieved.[3] Moreover, once unitary status is achieved in these areas and the desegregation decree is removed, the school district is not required to do anything to maintain integration so long as it does not intentionally recreate segregation.[4] A year later, in *Freeman v. Pitts* (1992), the Supreme Court revised the definition of unitary status. They replaced the old standard from *Swann v. Charlotte-Mecklenburg Board of Education*, namely, the elimination of "all vestiges of past discrimination," with the elimination of vestiges of past discrimination "to the extent practicable."[5] The Court then defined "the extent practicable" in terms of "good faith compliance" with existing desegregation decrees.[6] Their application of this definition in the case *Freeman v. Pitts* showed that this new interpretation of unitary status was very weak, indeed.[7]

Second, in *Missouri v. Jenkins* (1995), the Supreme Court further eroded the power of judicial desegregation decrees by deciding that the primary goal of any judicial desegregation decree was not to integrate schools, as one might expect, but to end court supervision of a school district as soon as possible.[8] Together, trends (1) and (2) have the result of rapidly bringing the era of court-ordered desegregation to a close in urban US school districts. Neither of these first two trends, however, directly affected those districts that operate desegregation programs voluntarily, without court supervision.

Third, since the late 1980s, the Supreme Court has begun to apply its toughest test, so-called "strict constitutional scrutiny," to all race-based classifications created by state governments (*City of Richmond v. J. A. Croson Co.* (1989)) and more recently to all governmental actions creating race-based classifications (*Adarand Constructors, Inc. v. Pena* (1995)). Former Justice Sandra Day O'Connor took pains to point out that it is not impossible in principle for some race-based classification to pass the strict scrutiny test. Nevertheless, in the four years between the Court's decision in *Adarand* and the decision by OPS to put a bond issue on the ballot in May 1999, the Court did not find any race-based classification that does pass the strict-scrutiny test.[9]

The Supreme Court did not have the opportunity to apply its strict scrutiny standard to a voluntary school desegregation program prior to May 1999, but other federal courts did. In 1998, the First Circuit Court of Appeals heard *Wessmann v. Gittens*, which challenged the Boston School Committee (BSC) policy of admitting students to its three exam, or magnet, schools on the basis of entrance exam scores together with "flexible racial/ethnic guidelines."[10] The Circuit Court handed down a split decision that placed an extraordinarily heavy burden of proof on the school district to show that vestiges of past discrimination still exist in Boston schools in order to justify the use of racial or ethnic guidelines in making admissions decisions.[11] Since the jurisdiction of the First Circuit Court of Appeals does not include Nebraska and since the BSC chose not to appeal the circuit court's decision to the Supreme Court, the decision in *Wessmann* did not apply directly to the OPS program of desegregation busing. But the *Wessmann* decision was clearly a bellwether decision for desegregation busing, as the OPS Board of Education noted in the Student Assignment Plan that it proposed in advance of the May 1999 bond issue election.[12]

Jurisprudence is not, of course, carried out in a social or political vacuum. The judicial trends I refer to have been fueled by growing opposition to affirmative action and related programs among white Americans. California's passage in 1996 of the anti-affirmative-action ballot initiative, Proposition 209, is only the most striking example of this political trend. On the left-liberal end of the political spectrum, the response to the right's backlash against government programs designed to redress race-related forms of injustice has largely been one of despair. Some legal commentators thought in the late 1990s that there were still grounds within current constitutional jurisprudence to wage a legal battle for school desegregation, but there was a notable lack of political will to carry out such a fight.[13]

It is in this legal and political environment that the Board of Education for Omaha Public Schools proposed to end desegregation busing in 1999. The OPS program of desegregation busing was initiated in 1975 by an Eighth Circuit Court of Appeals ruling that OPS actions related to student assignment led naturally and foreseeably to creating or maintaining segregated schools in five different areas of Omaha.[14] After further litigation, OPS hammered out a student assignment plan that was acceptable to both the Federal District Court of Nebraska and the Eighth Circuit Court, and busing began in the fall of 1976. The school district remained under court supervision until 1984, when the District Court determined that OPS had achieved unitary status.[15] The Board of Education then determined that OPS remained morally obliged to continue desegregation busing despite the lifting of the court order. The board continued the busing program voluntarily for fifteen years.

In 1998, the Board decided to revisit the decision to continue desegregation busing. By this time, the Supreme Court, under the leadership of Chief Justice William Rehnquist, had clearly turned the legal tide away from requiring desegregation busing in many cities and toward possibly forbidding it in some circumstances. As in US political culture at large, there were numerous voices on the OPS Board strongly opposing the continuation of desegregation busing. OPS conducted a survey of students' parents and found strong, across-the-board support for ending desegregation busing not only among whites but also among African-Americans. Around the time that the Board began holding public forums on the question of whether to end desegregation busing, the First Circuit Court handed down its decision in *Wessmann*.

At this point, the OPS Board of Education could read the writing on the wall. They saw that by the fall of 1999, the Supreme Court might issue a ruling upholding the First Circuit decision in *Wessmann*.[16] Such a decision could be used as precedent for a lawsuit challenging desegregation busing in OPS as employing an unconstitutional race-based classification for the purposes of student assignment. Such a lawsuit would have been difficult to defend against in the existing legal climate, especially given the lack of political will among OPS Board members to support the ideal of integration. Such a lawsuit would have been costly to fight and disastrous to lose. If OPS had been ordered to end desegregation busing and return to neighborhood schools in, say, the fall of 2000, most African-American elementary students living in the near north side would have attended school in the oldest, most dilapidated buildings in the district, several of which were ninety or more years old. This would have marked a return to the bad old days of separate and unequal in OPS, a result that OPS Superintendent John Mackiel expressly refused to accept. In order to avoid this worst-case scenario, Mackiel devised the 1999 OPS Student Assignment Plan

(SAP) and the accompanying bond issue proposal as a way of purchasing distributive justice for Omaha schools at the cost of school integration.

I accept what I take to be Mackiel's view of the legal situation, namely, that it is unlikely that anyone in Omaha had the power to forestall the end of desegregation busing in OPS for more than a couple of years. Effectively the question was not whether desegregation busing should end, but when and how it should end.[17] In retrospect, the end of integrated public education in Omaha has been a great loss because it has deprived white and non-white citizens of their primary opportunity to learn to interact with members of races other than their own. My aim in this chapter, however, is not to defend school integration as a valuable ideal, but to examine how best to work against white supremacy in the field of education in light of the demise of school integration in the US.

2. From Integration to Distributive Justice

The new SAP that went into effect in the fall of 1999 allows parents of OPS students, regardless of race, to send their children to their neighborhood school or, if they wish, to apply to send them to another nearby school in their zone or to one of the district's magnet schools.[18] The new SAP marked the end of a busing plan under which white students were bused out of their neighborhoods for one year and African-American students were bused out of their neighborhoods for at least three and more often five years between grades two and eight.[19] It also marked the first time that enrollment in all OPS magnet schools is open to African-American students: previously, students outside the local attendance area were eligible for admission to most magnet schools only if they were white, in order to promote racial balance. Many African-American parents viewed both of these developments as positive. Nevertheless, a third projected result of the 1999 SAP was that approximately 63% of African-American elementary students would attend schools with an African-American student population that is 20% or more higher than the district average.[20] Clearly the days of public school integration are past in Omaha, Nebraska.[21] Unsurprisingly, many African-American parents were wary of what this return to racially unbalanced schools might mean for their children.

Superintendent Mackiel's greatest fear, which he expressed in at least one public forum on the bond issue, was that these African-American students would return to crumbling schools on the near north side. So in return for giving OPS parents, and in particular white parents, the end to busing that they said they wanted, he asked them to pass a bond issue in the amount of $254 million. Over $200 million of this money was targeted for the construction of new neighborhood schools required by the SAP and the renovation and repair of aging schools. Over 90% of this money would be spent east of the 72nd Street boundary that divides the older, more racially diverse east side of town from the newer, predominately white west side of town. Nearly all of that 90% would go for renovation and repair of old buildings. The remainder of the money spent east of 72nd Street would go toward the creation of so-called academy schools with reduced class sizes in certain inner-city schools with poor achievement records.

The guiding ideal of the bond issue proposal seemed to be that if different races of students were to have separate schools, then the school district had to ensure that those separate schools got fair shares of the resources they needed to provide every student with an equal education. Thus the 1999 OPS bond issue marked a shift in the school district's interpretation of its state mandate to provide equal education to all students. This mandate is no longer understood to focus on school integration, but rather on fair distribution of resources among largely segregated schools.

The OPS School Board likely understood the old ideal of integration to be good in two distinct ways. (1) Integration is an educational good in itself, insofar as it permits students to learn in an environment that is significantly more diverse than the segregated neighborhoods in which most of them live. (2) Integration is an instrumental educational good, insofar as it ensures that a significant number of white parents, who have both more wealth to invest in their children's schools and more political clout with school administrators and the School Board, will have children in each school in the district. In this way, integration is instrumental to the goal of fair distribution of educational resources. In revising its interpretation of the ideal of equal education for all students from an ideal of integration to an ideal of fair distribution of educational resources, the Board was thus giving up on both (1) as an intrinsic good and (2) as a means of achieving fair distribution. The loss of (1) would be felt by all students, regardless of race, since all would benefit from exposure to a more diverse learning environment. But the loss of (2) would be a greater burden on members of non-white students, who would be more likely to receive an unfairly small share of the District's educational resources as a result.

It is difficult to maintain distributive justice between schools when the schools in question are not integrated. Given the vast disparity in income and wealth between whites, on the one hand, and African-Americans and Latinos, on the other, white parents can be expected to have significantly more money and leisure time on average to invest in their children's schools through PTAs and other avenues.[22] Studies also suggest that a wide array of obstacles impede non-white parents from participating effectively in their children's education when they do have the time.[23] So while OPS officials touted increased parental involvement in school activities as a primary benefit of returning to neighborhood schools, schools with predominately white student populations were more likely to reap these benefits than other schools. For these reasons, even an understanding of equal educational opportunity that is purely distributive in nature cannot currently be fully achieved without school integration in US cities where extensive residential segregation by race is a fact of life.

3. The Limits of Distributive Justice

Is an interpretation of the ideal of equal education stated purely in terms of distributive justice an adequate interpretation? Is fair distribution of educational resources among all the schools in a district enough to guarantee equal educational opportunity for the students in each of those schools? The ideal of fair distribution of educational resources will be difficult or impossible to attain in a largely segregated school district. But even if distributive justice were fully achieved, would that achievement exhaust what justice requires of a school district that has a legal mandate to provide equal educational opportunity to all its students? In what follows I will argue that it would not, for both theoretical and contextual reasons.

I argued in chapter four that a liberal theory of social justice that operates within the distributive paradigm will be inadequate to address the full variety of forms of social injustice that are related to white supremacy and patriarchy. Liberals who are committed to the distributive paradigm of social justice are, I argued, committed to an understanding of social justice as the social conditions required for the existence of autonomy, and to an individualistic social ontology and a distinction between choices and circumstances that are logically linked to the concept of autonomy. These theoretical commitments of liberals who operate within the distributive paradigm prevent them from addressing the functioning of white supremacist and patriarchal controlling images as forms of injustice. To address such forms of social injustice, I argued, we need to develop a successor political theory that is not committed to conceiving personal freedom as autonomy.

The purpose of this chapter is to illustrate the practical force of the theoretical critique of the distributive paradigm of social justice that I offered in chapter four and to explore how a successor political theory might conceive of social justice in terms that are not exclusively distributive. I will illustrate and explore these ideas in the particular historical context of public primary and secondary education in Omaha. Examining the details of this particular historical context will eventually lead to some broader theoretical insights, but in order to achieve these insights I need to look at the historical details first.

The distributive paradigm of social justice views schools within the OPS system as sites to which educational resources can be distributed and where equal educational opportunity can be created for individual students. It does not understand these schools as locations that have meaning within the specific social and cultural context of the history of race relations in Omaha. From the 1930s through the 1960s, the near north side of Omaha was a red-line ghetto for African-Americans. The Fair Housing Act of 1968 forced an end to legal residential segregation, but nearly forty years later it continues to be difficult for African-American families to find housing outside the old red lines. Today, Omaha's African-American population, which makes up the bulk of Nebraska's African-American population, remains concentrated in the near north side. This has resulted in the political isolation of African-Americans in city and state politics, where their interests are represented, in effect, by two school board members (out of twelve), one city councilor (out of seven) and one state senator (out of forty-nine).[24]

The political isolation of African-Americans in Omaha has made it difficult for them to resist the unjust treatment they have historically received at the hands of Omaha's city government, which generally serves the interests of Omaha-based multinational corporations and predominately white suburbanites employed by those corporations. North Omaha is now merely a shell of its former social, cultural, and commercial self as a result two major events that unraveled the fabric of the old neighborhood.

First, a series of riots in north Omaha in the late 1960s left the North 24th Street commercial corridor in shambles. As elsewhere in the US, these riots were caused by young African-Americans' general dissatisfaction with their social and economic conditions and race relations in the US.[25] But Omaha's city fathers directly contributed to at least one major riot by allowing segregationist Presidential candidate George Wallace to speak at Omaha's Civic Auditorium, located on the northern edge of downtown, just south of the near north side. This speech sparked a police riot against anti-Wallace demonstrators, which precipitated another riot in north Omaha the following night.[26]

Second, the city government backed the construction of the North Freeway in the early 1970s as a means of enabling white professionals to travel quickly between predominately white, suburban northwest Omaha and the downtown business district while bypassing African-American residential neighborhoods. This construction project required the destruction of miles of African-American residential neighborhoods and the division of the near north side into two disjoint parts with the new freeway as a boundary. The freeway construction project dragged on for thirty years while the property values of African-American homeowners displaced by the project deteriorated. Most African-Americans accepted the project as inevitable when it was first proposed in the 1950s, but many came to oppose it vocally by the time it neared completion in the 1970s.[27]

Omaha's city government has twice applied for and received federal money to repair the damage it helped to inflict on north Omaha. Twice it diverted that money to other uses. In the 1970s, the city obtained community development funding from the federal government on the condition that its use be determined through extensive consultation with community groups. The consensus among the community groups consulted was that the money should be used for urban renewal, particularly on the near north side. Nevertheless, Omaha City Council decided to use the funds for the construction of a grassy pedestrian mall with an artificial lake in the downtown business district, near the headquarters of US West Communications, the Union Pacific Railroad, ConAgra Foods, and First National Bank of Omaha. Again in the mid-1990s, the city obtained federal funding for the renewal of blighted areas on behalf of an area largely comprised by the near north side. The city diverted this money to the construction of an information systems research park in south-central Omaha for the benefit of First Data Resources.[28]

The history of black-white relations in Omaha is a repeating cycle: whites prey upon blacks; whites promise to repair the harm they have done; then whites betray those promises when the opportunity to benefit white suburbanites or a white-run corporation comes along. In the context of this history, it is no wonder that the first reaction of most African-American Omahans to the promise of any white city official is to expect him to do exactly the opposite of what he says.

This historical context of racial injustice was very much on the minds of the seventy-five or so people in attendance at a public forum on the OPS Bond Issue held on April 19, 1999, at Mt. Nebo Baptist Church, a predominately African-American church on the near north side. The event at Mt. Nebo was one of two public forums sponsored by an interfaith community action coalition called Omaha Together One Community (OTOC) in the weeks preceding the May 1999 Bond Issue vote.[29] The OTOC Public Forum at Mt. Nebo was the first time OPS Superintendent John Mackiel and the Yes for Kids campaign presented the proposed SAP and bond issue to near north side voters since its publication in January 1999.

OTOC leaders warned Mackiel that he should expect to face intense skepticism and outright hostility in the predominately African-American audience at Mt. Nebo, but he was undeterred. He began the meeting by making a brief sales pitch for the Bond Issue which stressed the benefits that north side schools could expect to receive in the form of renovated and repaired buildings and smaller class sizes.[30] Then, trusting in his ability to speak smoothly about the SAP and the Bond Issue off-the-cuff, he opened the floor for questions, and the deluge began. Anger seethed in the voices of audience members as they demanded that Mackiel address a long list of their historical grievances against OPS. Some of the issues that came up most frequently in ninety-minute-long barrage of questions included the following.

First, why, twenty-two years after the desegregation of OPS teaching assignments under the court order, were members of racial minorities, African-Americans and Latinos in particular, drastically underrepresented among OPS teaching and administrative staff? Why wasn't at least some of the money from the Bond Issue earmarked for recruitment and retention of non-white teachers?

Second, what would be done about the serious safety concerns about several school buildings on the near north side, and especially about the alarmingly high levels of lead discovered on some parts of the grounds of Druid Hill Elementary? How could parents be assured that all these conditions would be fully addressed by the time SAP implementation begins in Fall 1999?

Third, why did OPS feel it was necessary to rush from the first public hearings on the question of whether to end desegregation busing in November and December 1998 to the release of an entirely new SAP and Bond Issue proposal in January 1999 to a vote on the Bond Issue in May 1999? Why was the vote not delayed until at least November 1999 in order to allow for a full, fair public review and debate of the SAP and the proposed Bond Issue?

Fourth, given the limited representation of minority racial groups on the Board of Education, why did OPS fail to involve the larger Omaha community in general and the most affected racial groups in particular in the development of the SAP and the proposed bond issue?

Fifth, how could OPS voters, especially in north Omaha, trust OPS to fulfill the promises of the 1999 Bond Issue when a main project of the 1988 Bond Issue, namely, the renovation of Miller Park Elementary on the near north side, was not yet underway over ten years after that vote?

Sixth, in short, why should African-American citizens trust the current OPS Superintendent and the current Board of Education any more than they have trusted the other white officials of the school district and the city who betrayed their interests time and again? What in the world could make a rational resident of north Omaha believe that the promised hundreds of millions of dollars in school renovation and repair and new hiring of teachers would not evaporate on the near north side and rematerialize west of 72nd Street or someplace else where it would benefit whites rather than African-Americans or Latinos?

Superintendent Mackiel had few convincing responses to any of these questions. In response to the first question, Mackiel attributed the shortage of persons of color among OPS teachers and administrators to the district's abysmally low salaries, which he blamed on state legislation limiting the amount of property taxes districts can levy without obtaining voter approval. He did not go on to explain why improvements to the salary structure were not written into the Bond Issue proposal. In response to the second question, Mackiel tried to assuage parents' fears about the extent of lead contamination at Druid Hill Elementary, but he did not convincingly explain how the district planned to ensure that all safety concerns at buildings across the district were addressed by the first day of school in August 1999. As the questions continued to mount, Mackiel quickly ran out of answers and grew discouraged. By the end of the evening he looked like a man who had taken a beating.

The night might have been a complete write-off from an OPS perspective had Brenda Council not stepped in at the very end of the question period to give a rousing defense of the Bond Issue. Council, one of the two most prominent African-American politicians in the state, long represented the near north side on City Council and twice ran for mayor, very nearly winning election in 1997. In her brief, impromptu remarks, she quickly fired the audience's imagination with the argument that the 1999 Bond Issue represented the near north side's last, best chance to repair their crumbling school buildings and to end the inequity of African-American students' being bused five years for every one year that white children are bused.

4. From Distributive Justice to Dialogical Justice

What lessons should we learn from this examination of the historical context of race relations in Omaha and the concerns that African-American citizens raised at the OTOC Bond Issue Forum at Mt. Nebo that arise in this context? As a beginning, it seems to me that the main concerns raised there were by and large legitimate. By this I do not mean that these questions constitute an argument that proves that the 1999 OPS Bond Issue proposal was a dead letter that failed to address adequately the leading issues of educational inequality in Omaha. Rather, these are good questions that needed to be answered if the bond issue was to be accepted as an adequate remedy for educational inequalities in Omaha.

Some of the questions asked at the Mt. Nebo Forum raised distributive issues not adequately addressed by the SAP and the Bond Issue proposal. The first and second questions, for instance, appeal to the idea that every student, regardless of race, has two rights, namely, the right to be educated by a teaching staff in which persons of her or his race are represented roughly in proportion to their share of the student population, and the right to be educated in a school where the building and grounds are safe.

These rights claims can be justified as specifications of the more fundamental right to an equal education. The first is implied by the right to receive an equal education because every student needs role models of her or his own race to affirm that she or he and members of her or his own race are able to learn and succeed in life. The second is implied by the right to an equal education because physical safety is a material precondition for receiving a good education. A school district can help to secure each of these rights through the allocation of sufficient resources to the recruitment of minority teachers and the creation of safe buildings and grounds.

In addition, the fifth and sixth questions in part express doubt that the promised redistribution of educational resources away from wealthy west Omaha to schools in need in north and south Omaha would take place in a timely fashion or even at all. In these respects, the Mt. Nebo Forum can be viewed as raising questions about distributive justice that are not addressed in the SAP and the Bond Issue. Insofar as this is the case, the questions raised at Mt. Nebo raise further demands for distributive justice, but do not take us beyond the scope of distributive justice.

The participants in the Mt. Nebo Forum also raised questions, however, that went beyond the bounds of distributive justice. The third, fourth, fifth, and sixth questions all revolve around two related issues, namely, the lack of a trust relationship between African-American citizens and white OPS officials and the lack of opportunity for African-American citizens to participate equally and effectively in the development of education policy in Omaha.

Many different kinds of questions pointed repeatedly to the same issue: white city officials had repeatedly violated the trust of African-Americans in Omaha and thereby created an adversarial relationship characterized by a deep, well-founded mistrust of white leaders by African-Americans. In the absence of a trusting relationship, there is no package of distributive goods, however enticingly presented, that white city officials could sell to African-Americans in Omaha. In fact, the more enticing the package of resources, the more likely African-American citizens are to suspect that the package is being offered as part of a con game that will somehow end up benefiting whites and doing African-Americans little good or even some harm.

This raises an important point of contrast between the distributive approach to social justice, which characterized the proposal of the Board of Education and Superintendent Mackiel's presentation of that proposal, and a dialogical approach to social justice. The distributive approach assumes that social justice ultimately boils down to questions of who gets how much of what resources. This approach suggests that in negotiating about matters of justice, the parties to the negotiation should propose fair schemes for distributing resources across society, and then seek rationally to persuade the other parties to the negotiation that these schemes are, in fact, fair. But the distributive approach to social justice does not give us much help in thinking about the historical context in which these negotiations take place, the power relationships between the parties to the negotiations, and what the relationships between these parties need to look like in order for the negotiations to achieve justice. The distributive approach to social justice could certainly condemn as unjust a negotiation where one party denied another's basic civil or political rights. But if nothing so egregious occurs, the distributive approach is left with little to say.

The dialogical approach to social justice, by contrast, is not limited to focusing on the fair distribution of income, wealth, opportunities, and resources among individuals in discussing social justice. Any aspect of social relations that affects the freedom or well-being of members of society can be raised as a concern relevant to social justice. In the case at hand, that would certainly include the history of race relations in Omaha, the relative marginalization and powerlessness of the African-American community in Omaha city politics, and the distrust of city officials that is so widespread among African-Americans in Omaha as a result of these first two factors. The dialogical approach emphasizes the importance of all participants in the dialogue working to understand all such factors through an open, free, equitable dialogue. The process of working through dialogue to understand what justice requires of society here and now is instrumentally valuable to ending historical patterns of marginalization, powerlessness, and exploitation. It is also intrinsically valuable as a necessary part of building trust relationships among the citizens who participate in the dialogue.

The best way for the OPS Board of Education to repair their broken relationship with their African-American constituents would have been to show respect for them as equal citizens by involving them and other concerned members of the community in the process of developing the SAP and the bond issue from the very beginning. Only by ceasing to focus on selling a package of distributive goods and starting to focus on building relationships through dialogue could OPS hope to develop a new approach to student assignment that might elicit a broad consensus from African-Americans and Latinos as well as whites.[31] The trust relationships that OPS needs must be built on the democratic foundation of an equal voice in policy development for all members of the community, and especially for the members of those groups who stand to be most adversely affected by the end of busing. Only in this way could African-Americans cease to be disgruntled consumers of educational resources doled out by OPS and begin to become equal partners in creating educational equality in Omaha schools.

By the time of the disastrous OTOC Public Forum at Mt. Nebo, however, the policy development stage was history and the election was only a few weeks away. It was too late for Superintendent Mackiel to change the way the SAP and the bond issue proposal had been developed, even if he wanted to. Nevertheless, the superintendent did his best to learn the hard lessons that first Mt. Nebo Forum had to teach. He came back to the bargaining table with OTOC and hammered out an amendment to the SAP that provided for an Equity Assurance Committee (EAC) that would oversee the implementation of the SAP and the Bond Issue. Most of the EAC's members would be selected by a wide variety of community organizations including the Black Baptist Ministerial Association, the Omaha chapters of the NAACP and the Urban League, and other African-American groups, as well as OTOC. The EAC would oversee implementation of the SAP and the bond issue proposal at every stage and would hold the Board of Education accountable for delays or broken promises. As the lead pastor of Mt. Nebo Baptist Church remarked, the EAC was OTOC's way of "praying for [the bond issue] with one eye open. We will support it, but we will be vigilant."

Superintendent Mackiel publicly announced his concession to OTOC at a second public forum ten days after the first, before a predominately white and Latino crowd of nearly 200 at St. Pius X Catholic Church in midtown Omaha. Five days later, OTOC publicly endorsed the Bond Issue, much to Mackiel's relief. The next week, the Bond Issue carried by a 3% margin, an exceedingly narrow margin in a city accustomed to passing school levies in landslides. It is likely that the superintendent's concession on the EAC issue and the resulting endorsement of the bond issue by OTOC helped to push the bond issue across the finish line to victory, although this would be difficult to prove empirically.

The passage of the revised bond issue that included a community-appointed EAC was a partial victory for social justice and democracy in Omaha. It was a victory because it addressed not only the pressing issues of fair distribution of educational resources, but also the need to build relationships of trust and accountability between city officials and African-American citizens. But this victory was partial both because it was purchased at the cost of the experience of diversity that integrated schools can provide and because it did not address the need for non-white citizens to attain a greater voice in designing educational policy.

While these are important reservations, it is important to keep things in perspective. With regard to first reservation, it is unlikely that anyone in Omaha could have done anything in 1999 to avoid the end of desegregation busing in the near future.[32] In that light, it hardly seems fair to fault the OPS Bond Issue for failing to reverse the national trend away from desegregation busing. With regard to the second reservation, the EAC itself provides a community voice only in policy implementation and not in policy development. Thanks in part to the diligent oversight of the EAC, OPS significantly improved its bond issue project completion track record by comparison with the projects funded by the 1988 OPS Bond Issue. By June 2007, OPS reported that all 4 high schools, all 4 middle schools, and 17 out of 21 elementary schools that were scheduled for renovation or new construction funded by the 1999 OPS Bond Issue had, in fact, been completed. Contracts for the renovation of the remaining 4 elementary schools were in the close-out phase.[33]

My final verdict on the 1999 OPS Bond Issue is certainly mixed. But the public debate surrounding the bond issue clearly demonstrates the problems that a distributive conception of social justice encounters when it is divorced from a strong emphasis on participatory democracy. Distributive justice is all to the good, but what is to be distributed, by whom, how, and when, can only be decided in public debate. Without the social dialogue between disparate social groups and the relationships of trust and accountability that come with such dialogue, distributive justice is not only difficult to attain but inadequate to address all the forms of social injustice that exist in contemporary American society.

What was true in the case of the 1999 OPS Bond Issue is generally true about proposals for creating distributive justice. Unless all members of the public have an equitable opportunity to participate in deliberations about what distributive justice requires, proposals about distributive justice will not adequately capture the needs of all members of society, especially the needs of subordinate and marginalized groups. Moreover, it is only through social dialogue about matters of justice that the variety of diverse groups that make up a pluralistic, multicultural society can build the relationships necessary to trust one another to be honest and forthright in carrying out agreements made during negotiations. Distributive justice can only begin to be achieved within a context of participatory democracy. Political theorists must therefore turn their attention away from devising detailed schemes for the distribution of social resources in abstraction from and in advance of pluralistic deliberation about matters of distribution. In theorizing justice, an understanding of participatory democracy must precede any discussion of distribution.

Notes

1. See, for instance, Seyla Benhabib, *Situating the Self: Gender, Community, and Postmodernism in Contemporary Ethics* (New York: Routledge, 1992); James Bohman, *Public Deliberation: Pluralism, Complexity, and Democracy* (Cambridge, Mass.: MIT Press, 1996); John S. Dryzek, *Deliberative Democracy and Beyond: Liberals, Critics, Contestations* (New York: Oxford University Press, 2000); Jürgen Habermas, *The Theory of Communicative Action*, 2 vol., trans. T. McCarthy (Boston: Beacon, 1984-1987); Anne Phillips, *Democracy and Difference* (University Park, Pa.: Pennsylvania State University Press, 1993); and Iris Marion Young, *Inclusion and Democracy* (New York: Oxford University Press, 2000).

2. Kevin M. Graham, "Participatory Democracy in an Age of Global Capitalism," in *The Problems of Resistance: Studies in Alternate Political Culture*, ed. Steve Martinot and Joy James (Amherst, N.Y.: Humanity Books, 2001), 155–68; Graham, "The Ideal of Objectivity in Political Dialogue: Liberal and Feminist Approaches," *Social Epistemology* 16, no. 3 (2002): 295–309.

3. *Board of Education of Oklahoma City v. Dowell* 498 U.S. 237 (1991). "Unitary status" is a technical legal term for the state of integration that a school district must achieve in order to be released from a judicial desegregation decree. The US Supreme Court laid out its definition of "unitary status" in *Green v. County School Board of New Kent County, Virginia*, 391 U.S. 430 (1968).

4. William L. Christopher, "Ending Court-Ordered Desegregation of School Systems," *School Law Bulletin* vol. 23, no. 4 (Fall 1992): 1–7.

5. *Freeman v. Pitts* 112 S.Ct. 1430 (1992); *Swann v. Charlotte-Mecklenburg Board of Education* 402 U.S. 1 (1971).

6. Christopher, "Ending Court-Ordered Desegregation," 2–5.

7. In *Freeman*, the Supreme Court decided that DeKalb County, Georgia schools had achieved unitary status in 1992 because there was a single year, 1969-70, in which the school district had achieved racial balance under its desegregation plan. In the intervening twenty-two years, the court ruled, the school district was prevented from achieving unitary status by demographic shifts in the county population and other factors. See Christopher, 3–5.

8. *Missouri v. Jenkins* 115 S.Ct. 2038 (1995). See Mark Hansen, "A Road No Longer Taken," *ABA Journal* 84, no. 2 (Feb. 1998): 28–29.

9. Erica J. Rinas, "A Constitutional Analysis of Race-Based Limitations on Open Enrollment in Public Schools," *Iowa Law Review* 82 (1997); 1501–34.

10. *Wessmann v. Gittens* 160 F.3d 790 (1st Cir. 1998).

11. "Constitutional Law – Affirmative Action – First Circuit Holds That Public Exam School Policy That Uses Race as an Admissions Factor Offends the Equal Protection Clause – *Wessmann v. Gittens* 160 F.3d 790 (1st Cir. 1998)," *Harvard Law Review* 112 (1999): 1789–90.

12. Omaha Public Schools, *The Student Assignment Plan, April 1999* (Omaha: Omaha Public Schools, 1999), http://www.ops.org/OPS/Portals/0/DISTRICT/StudentAssignmentPlan/full-plan.pdf (accessed Jun. 14, 2007), 7–8.

13. See, for instance, "The Constitutionality of Race-Conscious Admissions Programs in Public Elementary and Secondary Schools," *Harvard Law Review* 112 (1999): 940–57.

14. *United States v. School District of Omaha*, 521 F.2d 530 (8th Cir. 1975). See Susan G. Clark, *The Judicial History of Desegregation in American Public Schools* (Ph.D. diss., Kent State University, 1997), 621–22.

15. Terry Hyland, "End of Court Supervision Changes Little at Schools," *Omaha World-Herald*, Sept. 17, 1984.

16. See Omaha Public Schools, *The Student Assignment Plan, April 1999*, 7–8. In the event, the Boston School Committee preempted Supreme Court action on the appeal of *Wessmann* by voting to end race-based student assignment on July 14, 1999. See Carey Goldberg, "Busing's Day Ends: Boston Drops Race in Pupil Placement," *New York Times* (July 15, 1999).

17. For all intents and purposes, the end of voluntary public school desegregation programs in the US came to an end when the US Supreme Court issued its 2007 decision in *Parents Involved in Community Schools v. Seattle School District No. 1*, 127 S. Ct. 2738 (2007). See James E. Ryan, "The Supreme Court and Voluntary Integration," *Harvard Law Review* 121 (2008): 131–56.

18. Omaha Public Schools, *The Student Assignment Plan, April 1999*, 10–12.

19. The 1999 SAP also had significant effects on the assignment of Latino students and the provision of English as a Second Language (ESL) services. In this chapter, however, I focus on the effects on African-American students both because the history of

anti-Black racism is much longer than that of anti-Latino racism in Omaha and because vocal opposition to the proposed SAP was much greater among African-Americans than among Latinos. Nonetheless, it is worth noting that predominately Latino precincts in South Omaha voted just as heavily against the 1999 OPS Bond Issue as predominately African-American precincts in north Omaha did.

20. In 2006, six years after the new SAP took effect, the actual figure was slightly lower: 58% of African-American elementary students in OPS attended schools with an African-American enrollment that was 20% or more higher than the district average. See Omaha Public Schools, "Official Fall, 2006 Membership Data" (Oct. 2006), 5–6.

21. In 1975, ten elementary schools, two junior high school, and one high school had predominately African-American enrollment (65% or more African-American enrollment). By 1987, ten years after busing began, only two elementary schools, no junior highs, and no high schools had predominately African-American enrollment. In 2006, six years after the new SAP came into effect, OPS reported that fourteen elementary schools, one middle school, and no high schools had predominately African-American enrollment. See "Busing in Omaha Brings Racial Balance," *Omaha World-Herald* (Nov. 15, 1987), and Omaha Public Schools, "Official Fall, 2006 Membership Data" (Oct. 2006), 5–6.

22. Racial disparity in income and wealth is commonplace across the US, but it is more extreme in Omaha than elsewhere. The US Census Bureau reports that in 2007 Omaha had the third-highest rate of African-American poverty and the highest rate of African-American child poverty in the US. See Henry J. Cordes, Cindy Gonzales, and Erin Grace, "Poverty amid prosperity: alarming figures reveal the reality of a metro area in which economic hardship has a stronger and stronger grip on the black community," *Omaha World-Herald* (Apr. 15, 2007).

23. Sheila M. Shannon, "Minority Parental Involvement: A Mexican Mother's Experience and a Teacher's Interpretation," *Education & Urban Society* 29, no. 1 (Nov. 1996): 71–84; Frances Gamer & Kathleen McCarthy Mastaby, "Parent Involvement in Urban Schools: The View from the Front of the Classroom," *New England Journal of Public Policy* 10, no. 1 (Summer-Fall 1994): 37–52; and Cathie Holden *et al.*, "Equally Informed? Ethnic Minority Parents, Schools and Assessment," *Multicultural Teaching* 14, no. 3 (Summer 1996): 16–20.

24. The concentration of many of Nebraska's African-American citizens in a single Omaha neighborhood also has the countertendency of concentrating African-Americans' political voice so that their concerns are at least heard, if not heeded. Two prominent African-American politicians, current State Senator Brenda Council and former State Senator Ernie Chambers, have made successful careers out of using this concentrated power to good ends.

25. See Hollis Limprecht, "Summer of 1966 was Long, Hot as the Riots Reached Omaha," *Omaha World-Herald*, June 16, 1985.

26. *Omaha World-Herald*, March 5 and 6, 1968.

27. "Chambers Seeks to Block Freeway Utility Payments," *Omaha World-Herald*, Aug. 6, 1983; "32 Year Project Divided Community. Is Freeway Progress? Some Still Unsure," *Omaha World-Herald*, Sept. 17, 1986; Howard Silber, "North Freeway May Clear Final Hurdles Next Year," *Omaha World-Herald*, Jul. 5, 1987.

28. Jena Janovy, "City Council Adopts Blight Resolutions," *Omaha World-Herald*, Dec. 18, 1996.

29. I have served in a variety of leadership positions in OTOC since 1997. My participation in the community organizing work of OTOC obviously affects my view of the events described in this chapter.

30. Pointedly absent from Superintendent Mackiel's remarks was any mention of a verbal agreement struck with OTOC earlier in the day to create an Equity Assurance Commission (EAC) made up of representatives of many community groups to oversee the implementation of the SAP and the projects funded by the bond issue.

31. When the 1999 OPS Bond Issue did receive voter approval by a narrow margin, it went down to defeat in both the near north side and in South Omaha. Many whites expressed amazement about this, since they saw the Bond Issue as designed for the benefit of African-American and Latino residents of these neighborhoods. These expressions of surprise betrayed a lack of understanding of the deep, well-founded mistrust of white city officials that was displayed so vividly at the Mt. Nebo Forum. See Paul Goodsell, "Affluent Suburbs Clinched Bond Vote," *Omaha World-Herald*, May 13, 1999.

32. In the long run, the most important factor in determining whether the new SAP can achieve educational equity in Omaha will probably be whether or not residential segregation by race can be ended in the Omaha real estate market, since this is now the only hope for integrated schools.

33. Omaha Public Schools, "Omaha Public Schools 1999 Bond Program," Mar. 1, 2006, http://www3.ops.org/bonds/Previoushome.html (accessed May 15, 2008).

Bibliography

32 Year Project Divided Community. Is Freeway Progress? Some Still Unsure. *Omaha World-Herald.* Sept. 17, 1986.

Abelmann, Nancy. *Blue Dreams: Korean Americans and the Los Angeles Riots.* Cambridge, Mass.: Harvard University Press, 1995.

Aiken, Linda H. and Douglas M. Sloane. Quality of In-Patient AIDS Care: Does Race Matter? Pp. 247–267 in *Problem of the Century: Racial Stratification in the United States,* edited by Elijah Anderson and Douglas S. Massey. New York: Russell Sage Foundation, 2001.

Alexander, Deborah. Civil Trial Pursued in Death: A Lawsuit by the Mother of Marvin Ammons, whom Police Shot in 1997, Goes to Trial Today. *Omaha World-Herald,* Apr. 8, 2000, Bulldog Edition.

———. "The Night Hangs in My Memory, Not Happily." A George Wallace Presidential Campaign Rally 30 Years Ago Sparked Four Days of Civil Unrest, Left One Person Dead and Polarized Omaha's Race Relations. *Omaha World-Herald,* Mar. 5, 1998, Metro Edition.

———. Officers Tell of Ammons Shooting: Sears' and Kister's Versions of Events Differ in the Men's First Public Testimony in the Death. *Omaha World-Herald,* Apr. 12, 2000, Sunrise Edition.

Alexander, Deborah, and Toni Heinzl. Jury Clears 2 Officers in Shooting. Lawyer: Verdict Means Claims Against City Will Be Dismissed. *Omaha World-Herald,* Apr. 14, 2000, Sunrise Edition.

Ansley, Frances Lee. Stirring the Ashes: Race, Class, and the Future of Civil Rights Scholarship. *Cornell Law Review* 74, no. 6 (Sept. 1989): 993–1077.

Appiah, Kwame Anthony. *The Ethics of Identity.* Princeton: Princeton University Press, 2005.

Baehr, Amy R. Toward a New Feminist Liberalism: Okin, Rawls, and Habermas. *Hypatia* 11, no. 1 (1996): 49–66.

Baehr, Amy R., ed. *Varieties of Liberal Feminism.* Lanham, Md.: Rowman & Littlefield, 2004.

Baldassare, Mark, ed. *The Los Angeles Riots: Lessons for the Urban Future.* Boulder: Westview, 1994.

Benhabib, Seyla. *Situating the Self: Gender, Community, and Postmodernism in Contemporary Ethics.* New York: Routledge, 1992.

Blum, Lawrence. *"I'm Not a Racist, But...": The Moral Quandary of Race.* Ithaca: Cornell University Press, 2002.

Bohman, James. *Public Deliberation: Pluralism, Complexity, and Democracy*. Cambridge, Mass.: MIT Press, 1996.

Brunkow, Angie. Access to Kruse Transcripts Denied: A Judge Turns Down a Prosecutor's Request for Grand Jury Documents in the Police Shooting of George Bibbins. *Omaha World-Herald*, Oct. 24, 2000, Sunrise Edition

——. Grand Jury Records Requested: County Attorney Seeks to Bolster Kruse Case. *Omaha World-Herald*, Sept. 15, 2000, Sunrise Edition.

——. Judge Seizes Reports in Ammons Shooting. *Omaha World-Herald*, Dec. 30, 1997, Sunrise Edition.

——. Kruse Charge Thrown Out: After a Manslaughter Count is Dismissed, the Case Continues with Selection of a Grand Jury in the Police Shooting. *Omaha World-Herald*, Aug. 19, 2000, Sunrise Edition.

——. Officer Sears Indicted: Grand Jury Charges Manslaughter in Ammons Death. *Omaha World-Herald*, Jan. 27, 1998, Sunrise Edition.

——. Sears Indictment Dismissed: Juror Misconduct Found. *Omaha World-Herald*, Nov. 6, 1998, Sunrise Edition.

——. Sears Lawyer Gets to Review Grand Jury Evidence. *Omaha World-Herald*, Jul. 2, 1998, Sunrise Edition.

Brunkow, Angie, and C. David Kotok. Ammons Jury Clears Officers. *Omaha World-Herald*, Jan. 21, 1999, Sunrise Edition.

——. Police Reports: Ammons had Loaded Gun in Hand. *Omaha World-Herald*, Jan. 1, 1998, Sunrise Edition.

Brunkow, Angie, and Karyn Spencer. No Indictment for Kruse: Despite Grand Jury Decision, Officer in Fatal Shooting May Still Face Charges. *Omaha World-Herald*, Sept. 2, 2000, Sunrise Edition.

Burbach, Chris. Alternate Juror Not One to Look the Other Way: The Ammons Case is not the First Time Pat Metoyer has Spoken Out When She Has Perceived Injustice. *Omaha World-Herald*, Nov. 8, 1998, Sunrise Edition.

Busing in Omaha Brings Racial Balance. *Omaha World-Herald*. Nov. 15, 1987.

Chambers Seeks to Block Freeway Utility Payments. *Omaha World-Herald*. Aug. 6, 1983.

Christopher, William L. Ending Court-Ordered Desegregation of School Systems. *School Law Bulletin* vol. 23, no. 4 (Fall 1992): 1–7.

Clark, Lorenne M. G. Women and Locke: Who Owns the Apples in the Garden of Eden? Pp. 16–40 in *The Sexism of Social and Political Thought: Women and Reproduction from Plato to Nietzsche*, edited by Lorenne M. G. Clark and Lynda Lange. Toronto: University of Toronto Press, 1979.

Clark, Lorenne M. G., and Lynda Lange, eds. *The Sexism of Social and Political Thought: Women and Reproduction from Plato to Nietzsche*. Toronto: University of Toronto Press, 1979.

Clark, Susan G. *The Judicial History of Desegregation in American Public Schools*. Ph.D. diss., Kent State University, 1997.

Collins, Patricia Hill. *Black Feminist Thought: Knowledge, Consciousness, and the Politics of Empowerment*. Boston: Unwin Hyman, 1990.

Constitutional Law – Affirmative Action – First Circuit Holds That Public Exam School Policy That Uses Race as an Admissions Factor Offends the Equal Protection Clause – *Wessmann v. Gittens* 160 F.3d 790 (1st Cir. 1998). *Harvard Law Review* 112 (1999): 1789–90.

The Constitutionality of Race-Conscious Admissions Programs in Public Elementary and Secondary Schools. *Harvard Law Review* 112 (1999): 940–57.

Cordes, Henry J., Cindy Gonzales, and Erin Grace. Poverty amid prosperity: alarming figures reveal the reality of a metro area in which economic hardship has a stronger and stronger grip on the black community. *Omaha World-Herald.* Apr. 15, 2007.

Crenshaw, Kimberlé, and Gary Peller. Reel Time/Real Justice. Pp. 56–70 in *Reading Rodney King: Reading Urban Uprising,* edited by Robert Gooding-Williams. New York: Routledge, 1993.

Delgado, Richard. Words that Wound: A Tort Action for Racial Insults, Epithets, and Name Calling. Pp. 89–110 55 in *Words that Wound: Critical Race Theory, Assaultive Speech, and the First Amendment,* edited by Mari J. Matsuda et al. Boulder: Westview, 1993.

Dryzek, John S. *Deliberative Democracy and Beyond: Liberals, Critics, Contestations.* New York: Oxford University Press, 2000.

Dworkin, Ronald. What is Equality? Part 1: Equality of Welfare. *Philosophy & Public Affairs* 10, no. 3 (1981): 185–246.

———. What is Equality? Part 2: Equality of Resources. *Philosophy & Public Affairs* 10, no. 4 (1981): 283–345.

Eiserer, Tanya, and Karyn Spencer. Officer Will Be Charged Today in Fatal Shooting. *Omaha World-Herald,* Jul. 26, 2000, Sunrise Edition.

Elshtain, Jean Bethke. *Public Man, Private Woman: Women in Social and Political Thought.* Princeton, N.J.: Princeton University Press, 1981.

Eze, Emmanuel Chukwudi, ed. *Race and the Enlightenment: A Reader.* Cambridge, Mass.: Blackwell, 1997.

Farber, Daniel A. *The First Amendment.* Second ed. New York: Foundation Press, 2003.

Frazer, Elizabeth, and Nicola Lacey. *The Politics of Community: A Feminist Critique of the Liberal-Communitarian Debate.* Toronto: University of Toronto Press, 1993.

Fuller, Janine, et al. *Restricted Entry: Censorship on Trial.* Vancouver: Press Gang, 1995.

Gamer, Frances, and Kathleen McCarthy Mastaby. Parent Involvement in Urban Schools: The View from the Front of the Classroom. *New England Journal of Public Policy* 10, no. 1 (Summer-Fall 1994): 37–52.

Garcia, J. L. A. Current Conceptions of Racism: A Critique of Some Recent Social Philosophy. *Journal of Social Philosophy,* vol. 28, no. 2 (Fall 1997): 5–42.

———. The Heart of Racism. *Journal of Social Philosophy,* vol. 27, no. 1 (Spring 1996): 5–45.

———. Philosophical Analysis and the Moral Concept of Racism. *Philosophy & Social Criticism,* vol. 25, no. 5 (1999): 1–32.

———. Racism and Racial Discourse. *The Philosophical Forum,* vol. 32, no. 2 (Summer 2001): 125–45.

Gates, Henry Louis, Jr. Parable of the Talents. Pp. 1–52 in Henry Louis Gates, Jr., and Cornel West, *The Future of the Race.* New York: Alfred A. Knopf, 1996.

Goldberg, Carey. Busing's Day Ends: Boston Drops Race in Pupil Placement. *New York Times.* Jul. 15, 1999.

Gonzalez, Cindy. Councilman Asks: Where Was Camera? Fatal Shooting Among Incidents Not Captured on Video, Brown Says. *Omaha World-Herald,* Oct. 30, 1997, Sunrise Edition.

———. Police Still Putting Together Events that Led to Shooting. *Omaha World-Herald,* Oct. 27, 1997, Metro Edition.

———. Police Union Defends Decision to Shoot. *Omaha World-Herald,* Nov. 4, 1997, Sunrise Edition.

Gonzalez, Cindy, and Chris Burbach. Black Leaders Voice Frustration. *Omaha World-Herald,* Jan. 21, 1999, Sunrise Edition.

Gooding-Williams, Robert, ed. *Reading Rodney King/Reading Urban Uprising*. New York: Routledge, 1993.

Goodsell, Paul. Affluent Suburbs Clinched Bond Vote. *Omaha World-Herald*. May 13, 1999.

Graham, Kevin M. The Ideal of Objectivity in Political Dialogue: Liberal and Feminist Approaches. *Social Epistemology* 16, no. 3 (2002): 295–309.

———. Participatory Democracy in an Age of Global Capitalism. Pp. 155–68 in *The Problems of Resistance: Studies in Alternate Political Culture*, edited by Steve Martinot and Joy James. Amherst, N.Y.: Humanity Books, 2001.

———. Race and the Limits of Liberalism. *Philosophy of the Social Sciences* 32, no. 2 (Jun. 2002): 219–39.

Green, Karen. Rawls, Women, and the Priority of Liberty. *Australasian Journal of Philosophy*, supp. vol. 64 (1986): 26–36.

Habermas, Jürgen. *The Theory of Communicative Action*, 2 volumes, translated by Thomas McCarthy. Boston: Beacon, 1984-1987.

Hansen, Mark. A Road No Longer Taken. *ABA Journal* 84, no. 2 (Feb. 1998): 28–29.

Hegel, G. W. F. *Lectures on the Philosophy of World History*. Trans. H. Nisbet. New York: Cambridge University Press, 1975.

Herrnstein, Richard J., and Charles Murray. *The Bell Curve: Intelligence and Class Structure in American Life*. New York: Free Press, 1994.

Holden, Cathie, et al. Equally Informed? Ethnic Minority Parents, Schools and Assessment. *Multicultural Teaching* 14, no. 3 (Summer 1996): 16–20.

Hyland, Terry. End of Court Supervision Changes Little at Schools. *Omaha World-Herald*. Sept. 17, 1984.

Jaggar, Alison. *Feminist Politics and Human Nature*. Totowa, N. J.: Rowman & Allanheld, 1983.

Janovy, Jena. City Council Adopts Blight Resolutions. *Omaha World-Herald*. Dec. 18, 1996.

Keller, Loren, and Cindy Gonzalez. Brown: Keep Cameras Rolling. *Omaha World-Herald*, Nov. 1, 1997, Sunrise Edition.

Kymlicka, Will. *Contemporary Political Philosophy: An Introduction*. Oxford: Oxford University Press, 1990.

———. *Liberalism, Community, and Culture*. Oxford: Clarendon, 1989.

———. Rethinking the Family. *Philosophy and Public Affairs* 20 (1991): 77–97.

Lawrence III, Charles R. If He Hollers, Let Him Go: Regulating Racist Speech on Campus. Pp. 53–88 in *Words that Wound: Critical Race Theory, Assaultive Speech, and the First Amendment*, edited by Mari J. Matsuda et al. Boulder: Westview, 1993.

Limprecht, Hollis. Centennial Series: Summer of 1966 Was 'Long, Hot' as the Riots Reached Omaha. *Omaha World-Herald*, Jun. 16, 1985, Sunrise Edition.

MacKinnon, Catharine. *Only Words*. Cambridge, Mass.: Harvard University Press, 1993.

Matsuda, Mari J. et al., eds. *Words that Wound: Critical Race Theory, Assaultive Speech, and the First Amendment*. Boulder: Westview, 1993.

Matsuda, Mari J. Public Response to Racist Speech: Considering the Victim's Story. Pp. 17–53 in *Words that Wound: Critical Race Theory, Assaultive Speech, and the First Amendment*, edited by Mari J. Matsuda et al. Boulder: Westview, 1993.

McGary, Howard. *Race and Social Justice*. Malden, Mass.: Blackwell, 1999.

Mill, Harriett Taylor. Enfranchisement of Women. Pp. 91–121 in *Essays on Sex Equality*, edited by Alice S. Rossi. Chicago: University of Chicago Press, 1970.

Mill, John Stuart. *On Liberty*, edited by Elizabeth Rapaport. Indianapolis: Hackett, 1978.

————. On the Grounds and Limits of the Laissez-Faire or Non-Interference Principle. Pp. 299–315 in *Reflections on Commercial Life: An Anthology of Classic Texts from Plato to the Present*, edited by Patrick Murray. New York: Routledge, 1997.

————. *The Subjection of Women*, edited by Susan Moller Okin. Indianapolis: Hackett, 1988.

————. *Utilitarianism*, second ed., edited by George Sher. Indianapolis: Hackett, 2001.

Mills, Charles. *Blackness Visible: Essays on Philosophy and Race*. Ithaca: Cornell University Press, 1998.

————. *From Class to Race: Essays in White Marxism and Black Radicalism*. Lanham, Md.: Rowman & Littlefield, 2003.

————. "Heart Attack": A Critique of Jorge Garcia's Volitional Account of Racism. *Journal of Ethics* 7 (2003): 29–62.

————. *The Racial Contract*. Ithaca: Cornell University Press, 1997.

Nielsen, Kai. *Equality and Liberty: A Defense of Radical Egalitarianism*. Totowa, N. J.: Rowman & Allanheld, 1985.

Nier III, Charles Lewis. Racial Hatred: A Comparative Analysis of the Hate Crime Laws of the United States and Germany. *Dickinson Journal of International Law* 13, no. 2 (Winter 1995): 241–79.

Njus, Elliot. "Lest We Forget" Our History. *Omaha World-Herald*, Jul. 15, 2009.

Nozick, Robert. *Anarchy, State, and Utopia*. New York: Basic Books, 1974.

Nussbaum, Martha. The Future of Feminist Liberalism. *Proceedings & Addresses of the American Philosophical Association* 74, no. 2 (2000): 59–67.

Okin, Susan Moller. Justice and Gender. *Philosophy & Public Affairs* 16 (1987): 42–72.

————. *Justice, Gender, and the Family*. New York: Basic Books, 1989.

————. *Political Liberalism*, Justice, and Gender. *Ethics* 105, no. 1 (Oct. 1994): 23–43.

————. Reason and Feeling in Thinking about Justice. *Ethics* 99, no. 2 (Jan. 1989): 229–49.

Oliver, Melvin L., and Thomas M. Shapiro. *Black Wealth/White Wealth: A New Perspective on Racial Inequality*. New York: Routledge, 1995.

Omaha Public Schools. *Official Fall, 2006 Membership Data*. Oct. 23, 2006. http://www.ops.org/OPS/LinkClick.aspx?link=RESEARCH%2fAdministrativeResearch%2f2006-2007_OfficialMembership2.pdf&tabid=284&mid=1343 (accessed Jun. 14, 2007).

————. Omaha Public Schools 1999 Bond Program. Mar. 1, 2006. http://www3.ops.org/bonds/Previoushome.html (accessed Jun. 13, 2007).

————. *The Student Assignment Plan, April 1999*. Apr. 1999. http://www.ops.org/OPS/Portals/0/DISTRICT/StudentAssignmentPlan/full-plan.pdf (accessed Jun. 14, 2007).

Outlaw, Lucius T., Jr. *On Race and Philosophy*. New York: Routledge, 1996.

Pateman, Carole. *The Sexual Contract*. Stanford, Calif.: Stanford University Press, 1988.

Pew Partnership for Civic Change. *Celebrating the Past – Charting the Future: Omaha's African American Community*. Omaha, Nebr.: Urban League of Nebraska, 2008.

Phillips, Anne. *Democracy and Difference*. University Park, Pa.: Pennsylvania State University Press, 1993.

Post, Robert, et al. *Prejudicial Appearances: The Logic of American Antidiscrimination Law*. Durham: Duke University Press, 2001.

Rawls, John. The Idea of Public Reason Revisited. *University of Chicago Law Review* 64 (1997): 765–807.

————. *Political Liberalism*. New York: Columbia University Press, 1993.

————. *A Theory of Justice*, rev. ed. Cambridge, Mass.: Harvard University Press, 1999.

Raz, Joseph. *The Morality of Freedom*. New York: Oxford University Press, 1986.

Rinas, Erica J. A Constitutional Analysis of Race-Based Limitations on Open Enrollment in Public Schools. *Iowa Law Review* 82 (1997): 1501–34.

Ring, Jennifer. Mill's *The Subjection of Women*: The Methodological Limits of Liberal Feminism. *Review of Politics* 47 (1985): 27–44.

Schwartzenbach, Sibyl. Rawls and Ownership: The Forgotten Category of Reproductive Labor. Pp. 139–167 in *Science, Morality, and Feminist Theory*, edited by Marsha P. Hanen and Kai Nielsen. *Canadian Journal of Philosophy*, supp. vol. 13 (1987).

Sen, Amartya. Well-being, Agency, and Freedom: The Dewey Lectures, 1984. *Journal of Philosophy* 82 (1985): 169–221.

Shannon, Sheila M. Minority Parental Involvement: A Mexican Mother's Experience and a Teacher's Interpretation. *Education & Urban Society* 29, no. 1 (Nov. 1996): 71–84.

Shapiro, Thomas M. *The Hidden Cost of Being African American: How Wealth Perpetuates Inequality*. New York: Oxford University Press, 2004.

Shelby, Tommie. Is Racism in the Heart? *Journal of Social Philosophy* 33 (2002): 411–20.

———. *We Who Are Dark: The Philosophical Foundations of Black Solidarity*. Cambridge, Mass.: Belknap Press of Harvard University Press, 2005.

Silber, Howard. North Freeway May Clear Final Hurdles Next Year. *Omaha World-Herald*. Jul. 5, 1987.

Smith, Anna Deavere. *Twilight – Los Angeles, 1992 on the Road: A Search for American Character*. New York: Anchor, 1994.

Sonenshein, Raphael J. *Politics in Black and White: Race and Power in Los Angeles*. Princeton: Princeton University Press, 1993.

Spelman, Elizabeth V. *Inessential Woman: Problems of Exclusion in Feminist Thought* Boston: Beacon, 1988.

Spencer, Karyn. Bibins Slaying Probe Inconclusive: A Police Investigation Finds Officer Jerad Kruse Thought the Chase Victim Had a Gun, But it Fails to Determine Whether the Shooting was Justified. *Omaha World-Herald*, Aug. 29, 2002, Metro Edition.

———. Pension Approved for Kruse. *Omaha World-Herald*, Aug. 17, 2001, Sunrise Edition.

———. Probe Under Way in Slaying by Police. *Omaha World-Herald*, Jul. 20, 2000, Sunrise Edition.

Spencer, Karyn, and Tanya Eiserer. Prosecutor Eyes Charges. Jansen: No Hasty Decision about Police Shooting. *Omaha World-Herald*, Jul. 21, 2000, Metro Edition.

Spencer, Karyn, Tanya Eiserer, and Henry J. Cordes. Dad: Kruse "Did What He Had To": Police Officer Charged in Shooting After Chase. *Omaha World-Herald*, Jul. 26, 2000, Metro Edition.

Strawbridge, Patrick, and Tanya Eiserer. Police Use of Deadly Force About Average: Fatal Police Shootings. *Omaha World-Herald*, Jul. 23, 2000, Sunrise Edition.

Tysver, Robynn. Kruse Can Be Charged, Court Says: But Grand Jury Transcripts in the Officer's Killing of George Bibbins Can't Be Reviewed by the Douglas County Attorney. *Omaha World-Herald*, May 31, 2002.

Tysver, Robynn, and Tom Shaw. Jansen: Kruse Won't Be Charged. The Decision Disappoints the Mother of George Bibins, the Man Killed by the Now-Retired Police Officer. *Omaha World-Herald*, Jun. 1, 2002, Sunrise Edition.

U.S. Bureau of the Census. *Fourteenth Census of the United States: State Compendium – Nebraska*. Washington, D.C.: U.S. Government Printing Office, 1925.

Webster, Bruce H., Jr., and Alemayehu Bishaw. *Income, Earnings, and Poverty Data from the 2006 American Community Survey*. Washington, D.C.: U.S. Government Printing Office, 2007.

Wollstonecraft, Mary. *A Vindication of the Rights of Woman*. New York: Penguin Books, 1992.

Young, Iris Marion. *Inclusion and Democracy*. New York: Oxford University Press, 2000.

———. *Justice and the Politics of Difference*. Princeton: Princeton University Press, 1990.

Index

Abbott, James F., 17
Adarand Constructors, Inc. v. Pena, 90
African-Americans, 42–44, 45–46; hate
    speech about, 77; social and eco-
    nomic standing of, 1, 10; white
    supremacist controlling images of,
    64–67, 78; *see also* controlling
    images; Omaha, Nebr.; Omaha
    Public Schools
Ammons, Marvin, 17–18, 19–24
Ansley, Frances Lee, 9
Appiah, Anthony, 42, 62, 65–67, 68;
    ethical individualism, 66–67, 68
autonomy, 53–59, 63–68

Bibins, George, 18–24
Blum, Lawrence, 7–8
*Board of Education of Oklahoma City
    v. Dowell*, 89
Boston School Committee, 90, 102n16

California Proposition 209, 90
Cedarville, Oh., xi–xii
Chambers, Ernie, 103n24
Charlotte-Mecklenburg, School District
    of, 89; *see also Swann v. Char-
    lotte-Mecklenburg Board of Edu-
    cation*
choice-circumstance distinction, 54,
    55–59
City of Richmond v. J. A. Croson Co.,
    90
Collins, Patricia Hill, xiv, 59, 71
controlling images, 59–61, 66–67, 71–
    72; Aunt Jemima, 82; black
    mammy, 78; black rapist, 61–62,

63–64; dragon lady, 60–61; Jeze-
    bel, 78; Negro/ape, 78, 79; Sambo,
    78; self-sacrificing mother, 60–61;
    white supremacist, 78–79, 82
Council, Brenda, 97, 103n24

desegregation busing, 88–89, 100; *see
    also* Omaha Public Schools
dialogical theory of social justice, 87–
    89, 97–99
distributive paradigm of social justice,
    54–55, 57, 63–67, 80, 84, 87–89,
    94, 97–99
Dworkin, Ronald, 54

education, anti-white supremacist, 59,
    61–63, 80
effects on speech, 76–77, 82–84; *see
    also* freedom of thought and ex-
    pression
Eighth Circuit Court of Appeals, 91
equality of resources, 54, 64
Eze, Emmanuel, 9

Federal District Court of Nebraska, 91
First Circuit Court of Appeals, 90
First Data Resources, 95
freedom of thought and expression, 71–
    72; *see also* effects on speech
Freeman v. Pitts, 89–90

Garcia, J. L. A., 2–7
*Green v. County School Board of New
    Kent County, Virginia*, 102n3

113

Breinigsville, PA USA
03 February 2010
231412BV00002BB/1/P